Cultural Materialism

Interpretations

This series provides clearly written and up-to-date introductions to recent theories and critical practices in the humanities and social sciences.

General Editors
Stephen Knight (De Montfort University)
and Ken Ruthven (University of Melbourne)

Advisory Board
Tony Bennett (Griffith University)
Penny Boumelha (University of Adelaide)
John Frow (University of Queensland)
Sneja Gunew (University of Victoria, British Columbia)
Robert Hodge (Murdoch University)
Terry Threadgold (Monash University)

Already published:
Cultural Materialism, by Andrew Milner
Metafictions?, by Wenche Ommundsen

In preparation:
Foucauldian criticism, by Alec McHoul and Wendy Grace
Framing and interpretation, by Gale MacLachlan and Ian Reid
Aboriginality, by Tim Rowse
Postmodern socialism, by Peter Beilharz
Multicultural literature studies, edited by Sneja Gunew
Post-colonial literary studies, by Anne Brewster

Cultural Materialism

Andrew Milner

MELBOURNE UNIVERSITY PRESS
1993

First published 1993
Designed by text-art
Typeset in 10½ point Garamond
Printed in Malaysia by
SRM Production Services Shd Bhd for
Melbourne University Press, Carlton, Victoria 3053
U.S.A. and Canada: International Specialized Book Services, Inc.,
5804 N.E. Hassalo Street, Portland, Oregon 97213-3644
United Kingdom and Europe: University College London Press,
Gower Street, London WC1E 6BT, U.K.

ISSN 1039-6128

National Library of Australia Cataloguing-in-Publication data

Milner, Andrew, 1950–
    Cultural Materialism.
    Bibliography.
    Includes index.
    ISBN 0 522 84493 6.
    1. Culture. 2. Economic anthropology. 3. Marxist anthropology. I.
    Title. (Series: Interpretations).

For Verity

Contents

Acknowledgements

As always, I am indebted to Verity Burgmann, for just about everything, but especially for bearing the brunt of the childcare during the school holidays. I am grateful to our sons, David and James, for handling the mothercare over approximately the same period. Friends, colleagues and students in the Monash University Centre for Comparative Literature and Cultural Studies and the University of Leeds Centre for Cultural Studies listened politely, and sometimes rudely, whilst I rehearsed these arguments. Staff at the Monash University Library and at the Brotherton Library, University of Leeds, were invariably helpful. Special thanks are due also to Sue Stevenson, who taught me how to use Wordperfect, and to Gaynor Thornell and Ros Shennan, for the loan of their printers. Stephen Knight and John Iremonger were interested and encouraging. Terry Eagleton and Colin Sparks made helpful comments on Chapter 4. Last but not least, thanks are due to John Forster, my Sixth Form English teacher, who first introduced me to Leavis, Williams and Hoggart, Liverpool poets, the Royal Shakespeare Company, Pelican Books and W. H. Smith's.

1

Introduction

We all know what 'culture' means: it is surely one of the most widely used abstract nouns available to our vocabulary. We worry about the independence of the Australian national culture; about whether we personally are sufficiently 'cultured' to 'get on' in life; about whether the feminist movement can promote a properly autonomous women's culture; about the possibility and desirability of living in a multi-cultural society; about the prospects for a 'culture-led' recovery in the Victorian economy (that is, if we happen to live in Melbourne). In my profession as a university teacher, I worry also about the administrative organisation of 'cultural studies' within the wider Faculty of Arts. The odd thing about these worries, however, is that they are each worryingly ambiguous. When we think of an independently Australian culture, we might well have in mind our own distinctive arts and literature, as embodied both in individual works, Patrick White's *Voss* for example, and in institutions, for example the Australian Opera, or even the Australia Council. But we might also be thinking much more generally of our distinctively Australian ways of doing things: the beach and the barbecue, mateship and machismo, *Hungry Jack's*, the arbitration system and Australian rules football. To be 'cultured' might mean to be able to spot intertextual references to T. S. Eliot; but it also might mean being able to affect a phoney English accent. A women's culture could mean books and paintings, and by extension independent publishing houses and galleries; or it could refer to entirely novel, radically cooperative and nurturing, ways of organising political, economic and domestic activitity. Multiculturalism might mean more Greek literature in schools, or more Italian films on SBS; but it might also mean significant modifications to those distinctively Australian ways of doing things, kebabs as well as steak, for example, or soccer instead of football. A 'culture-led' economic recovery probably would have something to do with *The Phantom of the Opera* or the Royal Melbourne Institute of Technology; but it might just mean that the Victorians should be persuaded to sell their way of life, for tourism, say, as do the Balinese and the Irish. As for cultural studies, for some it quite clearly means the classics, fine arts, and the high literary canon; and for others the sociology of adolescent gang warfare and the anthropology of kinship. The problem, of course, is that we all mean a great deal more than we know.

Culture, observed Raymond Williams, the Welsh cultural theorist, 'is one of the two or three most complicated words in the English language' (Williams, 1976a:76). That complexity is nowhere more apparent than in Williams's own attempts to define its usage. In his first major work, *Culture and Society*, he drew attention to four important kinds of meaning which attach to the word, referring respectively to: an individual habit of mind; the state of intellectual development of a whole society; the arts; and finally, the whole way of life of a group or people (Williams, 1963:16). In the later *Keywords*, itself originally intended as an appendix to *Culture and Society*, but significantly amended and augmented thereafter, only the latter three usages remain in play (Williams, 1976a:80). Later still, his sociology textbook, *Culture*, would reintroduce the first usage, grouping it together with the second and third as 'general', and contrasting these with the fourth, more specifically 'anthropological' meaning (Williams, 1981:11). Williams distinguishes also between the word's physical and human applications; between its positive and negative connotations; its use as a noun of process and as a noun of configuration; its politically radical and politically reactionary applications; and so on. The confusions and complications belong to our 'culture' itself, if we may so use the word, rather than to any fault in Williams. For, as he himself observes: 'These variations . . . necessarily involve alternative views of the activities, relationships and processes which this complex word indicates. The complexity, that is to say, is not

. . . in the word but in the problems which its variations of use significantly indicate' (Williams, 1976a:81).

For all these variations both in common usage and in Williams's own, the distinction which most fascinates him is that between its literary-critical and aesthetic applications on the one hand, and its sociological and anthropological on the other. Neither of these can be considered distinctively 'general', despite Williams's occasional observations to the contrary. But both extend well beyond the boundaries of any particular academic discipline. Thus:

> the concept of 'culture' . . . became a noun of 'inner' process, specialized to its presumed agencies in 'intellectual life' and 'the arts'. It became also a noun of general process, specialized to its presumed configurations in 'whole ways of life'. It played a crucial role in definitions of 'the arts' and 'the humanities', from the first sense. It played an equally crucial role in definitions of the 'human sciences' and the 'social sciences', in the second sense. (Williams, 1977a:17)

Culture, then, may be counterposed to society, as 'art'; but the two may also be defined very nearly coextensively, as the non-political, non-economic, residually 'social'. The conjunction in the title *Culture and Society* is thus no less ambiguous a term than either of the nouns: it can imply an essentially external relation of aggregation or opposition; or, conversely, an essentially internal relation of near inclusion.

This most fundamental ambiguity, that between culture as art and culture as society, arises very directly from out of the deep structures of the modern world. It is only in societies roughly similar to our own, that is, in those constructed politically as democratic or quasi-democratic nation states, and economically as industrial or industrialising, capitalist or state capitalist, that 'culture' and 'society' become excluded from both politics and economics. In pre-modern societies, such as those of pre- conquest Australia, or indeed those of medieval Europe, the business of government, as also the business of work, is properly understandable only as an integral part of a wider culture, part of a wider society. That this is so is most clearly attested to by the absolutely central position occupied by religious belief and practice in both instances: neither a corroboree nor a coronation can be imagined other than as in some sense a significantly religious event. The ambiguities in the terms culture and society, and in their mutual relations, as also the very currency of both terms in contemporary discourse, bear witness to the deeply problematic status of each in a society whose driving imperatives are characteristically secular, political and economic. This process, by which 'culture', and with it 'society', become the more theoretically and discursively salient the more they are effectively extruded from the 'practical' business of life, is nicely caught in Williams's own account of the evolution of the concept 'culture' in nineteenth–century English thought. Culture, he observes, emerged

> as an abstract and an absolute: an emergence which . . . merges two general responses—first, the recognition of the practical separation of certain moral and intellectual activities from the driven impetus of a new kind of society; second, the emphasis of these activities, as a court of human appeal, to be set over the processes of practical social judgement and yet to offer itself as a mitigating and rallying alternative. (Williams, 1963:17)

Culture thus understood, that is, as separate from and superior to both economics and politics, is initially the creation of European Romanticism. As such, it denotes the arts, and perhaps especially literature. 'Poets are the unacknowledged legislators of the world', wrote Shelley (1931:109). But the importance of art, and the ultimate legislative power of poetry, reside in their status as an expression of the distinctive 'spirit' of a people. Thus, art as 'culture' is counterposed to the mechanism of modern industrial 'civilisation'. This more properly 'social' sense of the term, already present in Romanticism, is finally foregrounded in the twin 'social sciences' of anthropology and sociology. For Emile Durkheim, the 'founding father' of French anthropology, it was the 'collective consciousness' of tribal culture which allowed us to distinguish most clearly between pre-industrial 'mechanical solidarity' and the 'anomie' of a modernity still chronically incapable of 'organic solidarity' (Durkheim, 1964:129–32, 353–73). For the early German sociologists, such as Max Weber and Ferdinand Tönnies, the opposition would run between status and class, *Wertrationalität* (value rationality) and *Zweckrationalität* (purposive rationality), *Gemeinschaft* (community) and *Gesellschaft* (association), feudalism and capitalism (Weber, 1948:180–95; Weber, 1964:115; Tönnies, 1955:37–9). In each case, modern society is understood as distinctively and unusually asocial, its economic and political life characteristically 'normless' and 'value-free', in short, uncultured.

This sense of culture as a superior ideal, informing the whole way of life of whole peoples, as a matter of fact in pre-modern societies, perhaps only ideally so within modernity itself, is ofen characterised as *idealist*. The latter term derives from philosophy and, in its more restricted uses, is applied to the 'classical idealism' of late eighteenth–century and early nineteenth–century German thought, most importantly to Kant and to Hegel. It is clear, however, that roughly analogous notions subsequently become central to the development of both English literary criticism and German sociology. The former is influenced by German idealism by way of English and German Romanticism—Coleridge remains a key figure here (Coleridge, 1972); the latter by way of a late nineteenth century revival in neo-Kantian philosophy; and the debt is very real in each case. This is much less obviously so for French anthropology: Durkheim's 'idealism' points forward to modern structuralism and semiotics, rather than back to Romanticism or German idealism. But in its implicit valorisation of tribal unity over industrial anomie, and in its location of the source of that unity in the collective consciousness, it significantly reproduces two of the characteristic tropes of Anglo-German idealism. Moreover, in its subsequent appropriation by British 'social anthropology', the Durkheimian corpus is significantly 'naturalised', and thereby subsumed into a wider idealist tradition.

The obvious contrary instance in modern western thought, that of a *materialism* stubbornly resistant to the lures of idealism, is provided by the British tradition of philosophical utilitarianism, and by its various intellectual progeny, notably the disciplines of economics and political science, but perhaps also behaviourist psychology. For Thomas Hobbes, the central seventeenth–century precursor of modern English political philosophy, the initial datum for any adequate understanding of human social behaviour was to be neither religion nor art, nor manners nor morals, nor anything else subsequently acknowledged as 'culture', but rather the physical movement of the material human body: 'life itself is but motion, and can never be without desire, nor without fear' (Hobbes, 1960:39). The body and its desires and fears, to pursue pleasure and to avoid pain, thus provide utilitarianism with a fundamental measure from which to deduce the nature of political and economic systems, both real and ideal. This has proven an immensely fertile intellectual enterprise, as the cumulative achievements of modern economic theory, to take the obvious example, clearly attest. But utilitarianism has proven almost entirely unsuccessful, by contrast, as a point of entry into the understanding and explanation of culture. This is so for the most obvious of reasons, that in a strictly utilitarian system there can be *no* culture, *no* society, but only a plurality of discrete individual actors connected to each other either through the immediately economic contracts of the marketplace or through the compulsions of the state, itself conceived as the effect of a supposedly pre-political 'social contract'. On this view, culture, whether understood as art or as society, is reduced to an aggregate of individual commodities, each for sale in the marketplace of individual taste, its value determined solely by the revealed preferences of the aggregate of individual cultural consumers. As the nineteenth–century utilitarian philosopher Jeremy Bentham insisted: 'push-pin is of equal value with . . . poetry' (Bentham, 1962:253).

A rigorous materialism, such as that proposed by Hobbes and subsequently pursued by modern economic theory, is thus fundamentally unable to conceive of the cultural as meaningfully distinguishable from the economic and the political. For it is in the nature of culture, as defined by both poetry and anthropology, that it possess both an internal order of its own and certain clearly coercive, or at least compulsive, properties *vis à vis* the individual. Culture *cannot* be reduced to a simple matter of individual preference, mere taste. 'Poetry is the most philosophic of all writing', writes Wordsworth, 'its object is truth, not individual and local, but general and operative' (Wordsworth, 1952:394); and later, 'the Poet binds together by passion and knowledge the vast empire of human society' (ibid.:396). For Durkheim, 'the collective consciousness is the highest form of the psychic life, since it is the consciousness of the consciousnesses . . . outside of and above local contingencies, it sees things only in their permanent and essential aspects, which it crystallizes into communicable ideas' (Durkheim, 1976:444). Doubtless, both Durkheim and

Wordsworth (and, indeed, Shelley) overstate their case. But, even if the truth of poetry is perhaps not quite so general, the unacknowledged legislature perhaps not quite so powerful, the consciousness of the consciousnesses perhaps not quite so permanent and essential, each sentiment nonetheless captures a part of what many of us experience as the most basic of truths about our 'culture': that our art, our religion, our morals, our knowledge, our science, are not simply matters of private preference, but rather possess an 'objectivity' the validity of which is barely touched upon by notions such as that of taste; in short, that we belong to our culture very much more than it belongs to us. It is this experience, this 'truth' if we like, which is radically unamenable to analysis in terms of the utilitarian schema. Whatever else utilitarian political economy may have achieved, it remains constitutionally incapable of an adequate theory of culture.

There are weaker versions of materialism, however, which insist not so much on the exclusion of the cultural as on its merely secondary character. The most important of these historically has been *Marxism*. There is a sense in which, as the American sociologist Talcott Parsons once observed, Marxism might well be considered simply a sub-variant of the more general utilitarian tradition (Parsons, 1949:110). But this is a part of the truth only, and the lesser part at that. In fact, Parsons's own clear lack of interest, even perhaps antipathy, leads him to a serious underestimation of the continuing debt owed by Marx both to German idealism and to Romanticism. Undoubtedly, the main trajectory of Marx's mature intellectual career is indeed best understood in its relation to the distinctively British tradition of utilitarian and quasi-utilitarian political economy. But his early intellectual formation had been shaped, nonetheless, by German Romanticism and by Hegelianism. The resultant synthesis, while increasingly conducted in the language of political economy, continues to rehearse a number of important idealist thematics, most obviously those present in the theories of alienation and 'commodity fetishism', and in the implicitly invidious comparison between use-value and exchange-value (Marx, 1975:327–30; Marx, 1970:71–83). Marx's *magnum opus* is thus not so much an extension as, in the words of its subtitle, a *critique* of political economy.

Marxian materialism is, in fact, able to reserve a place for culture, albeit, in the more historically persuasive formulations, an essentially secondary one. The best known of these, and almost certainly also the most influential, is the so-called base/superstructure formula, in which 'the economic structure of society' is deemed 'the real foundation', which gives rise to a legal and political 'superstructure', and thence to correspondent 'definite forms of social consciousness' (Marx, 1975:425). These latter, which are described as 'religious, artistic or philosophic' (ibid.:426), are not specifically defined as superstructures by Marx himself, but the elision routinely occurs in most subsequent 'scientific' Marxisms. Obvious instances here include the Russian Marxists Georgei Plekhanov (Plekhanov, 1978) and, rather more ominously, Andrey Zhdanov (Zhdanov, 1977). Less well known internationally, but of greater local significance to the English-speaking world, were the British Marxist literary critics Christopher Caudwell and Ralph Fox (Caudwell, 1946; Fox, 1979). Here, as elsewhere in 'scientific socialism', the separate existence of culture as a 'relatively autonomous' realm, neither directly reducible to nor coextensive with the economy, is readily conceded. But its role remains epiphenomenal, an adjunct to, effect of, or even, in Caudwell's unfortunate phrase, a 'secretion' from (Caudwell, 1946:29), the 'economic base'.

For much of the twentieth century, cultural theory has been polarised between idealist accounts, most obviously those proposed by traditional literary humanism, but also those deployed in both post-Weberian sociology and post-Durkheimian anthropology, and materialist accounts, normally of a specifically 'vulgar' Marxist kind. Comparing such idealisms and materialisms, Williams observes that

> the importance of each position . . . is that it leads . . . to intensive study of the relations between 'cultural' activities and other forms of social life . . . The sociology of culture, as it entered the second half of the twentieth century, was broadly compounded of work done from these two positions. (Williams, 1981:12)

In the 1960s and 1970s, however, there were also brought into play, in both Britain and France, new theoretical paradigms which sought, rather, to establish the materiality of culture itself. Williams continues:

> a new kind of convergence is becoming evident . . . it differs in its insistence that 'cultural practice' and 'cultural production' . . .

are not simply derived from an otherwise constituted social order but are themselves major elements in its constitution . . . it sees culture as the *signifying system* through which necessarily . . . a social order is communicated, reproduced, experienced and explored. (ibid.:12–13)

Williams himself could write with peculiar authority on this subject quite simply because his own work had come to provide the paradigmatic instance, in the English-speaking world at least, of precisely that new kind of convergence. The term 'cultural materialism' was coined by Williams to denote his own break from an older tradition of British Communist Marxism on the one hand and that distinctly British version of literary humanism associated above all with the work of his own former teacher, the literary critic F. R. Leavis, on the other. But the term can easily be used more generally to describe this emergent body of cultural theory. It is that convergence, and more particularly Williams's own contribution therein, which provide this book with its central subject matter.

What exactly are we to understand by the term 'cultural materialism'? Williams himself first used it in a short essay published in the hundredth issue of the journal *New Left Review*, to which he had been a longstanding contributor. Cultural materialism, he explained,

is a theory of culture as a (social and material) productive process and of specific practices, of 'arts', as social uses of material means of production (from language as material 'practical consciousness' to the specific technologies of writing and forms of writing, through to mechanical and electronic communications systems). (Williams, 1980:243)

The position would be 'spelled out more fully', he added, in *Marxism and Literature* and in the book that would eventually be published as *Culture* (ibid.). There is an important sense in which these two books do indeed 'spell out' the theory, and they will, then, command much of our attention in the pages that follow, most especially in chapter three, where Williams's cultural materialism is elaborated upon in some detail. But we should note also Williams's own insistence, in the Introduction to *Marxism and Literature*, that cultural materialism had been 'a position which, as a matter of theory,

I have arrived at over the years' (Williams, 1977a:5). Its pre-history, as part of a much longer intellectual evolution, demands our attention also. That history, as articulated both in Williams's own work and in that of his more directly relevant predecessors and contemporaries, will be surveyed in the chapter which immediately follows. Chapter two, then, will be devoted to the extremely complex question of Williams's earlier 'left culturalism', and of its doubly ambivalent relationship to Leavisism on the one hand, Marxism on the other. That such a legacy exists seems incontrovertible: as late as 1979, and while commenting on *Marxism and Literature*, Williams would still insist that 'I was trying to say something very much against the grain of two traditions, one which has totally spiritualized cultural production, the other which has relegated it to secondary status' (Williams, 1979a:352–3). Williams's initial negotiation of this relationship finds expression most importantly in *Culture and Society*, first published in 1958, and *The Long Revolution*, published in 1961. These two works will provide a central focus for our second chapter. But Williams was by no means working in an intellectual or political vacuum. His reaction against Leavisism had been shared, in part at least, by Richard Hoggart; that against Communist Marxism by E. P. Thompson. Their work, as also the wider context of the radical intellectual culture of the 1950s and early 1960s, will require some further examination at this point.

In *Marxism and Literature*, Williams describes cultural materialism as 'a theory of the specificities of material cultural and literary production within historical materialism' (Williams, 1977a:5). This latter term is Marx's, and it therefore comes as little surprise that Williams should here view cultural materialism as 'in my view, a Marxist theory, and indeed . . . in its specific field' as 'part of what I at least see as the central thinking of Marxism' (ibid.:5–6). We are under no obligation, however, to concur in this judgement. Tony Bennett, for example, has recently sought to establish not only that there is nothing especially Marxist about cutural materialism, but also that other intellectual traditions, most notably feminism and Foucauldian post-structuralism, are actually more properly 'historical materialist' than is Marxism itself (Bennett, 1990:13–14, 35–6). From a position much more sympathetic to Marx, and to the base/superstructure metaphor, Terry Eagleton has argued that Williams's cultural materialism is not so much non-Marxist as pre-Marxist: 'it returns us back *before* Marx's full development of historical materialism, to the earlier philosophical contentions between materialism and idealism' (Eagleton, 1989a:169). In an obituary written shortly after Williams's death, Nicholas Garnham, one of his very few occasional co-authors (Garnham and Williams, 1986), and indeed a self-confessed cultural materialist in his own right (Garnham, 1983), chose to stress that 'Williams's importance lies precisely in his at times highly critical but nonetheless lifelong allegiance . . . to historical materialism as an intellectual project' (Garnham, 1988:130). Clearly, the connection between Williams's cultural materialism and other materialisms, historical and otherwise, remains a matter for some considerable controversy, not least in the ranks of his own admirers, among whom one could count Bennett, Eagleton and Garnham. The point at issue here is most certainly not Marxism as it had been understood by the Communists, but rather a whole series of much more recent, and in truth much more intellectually interesting, materialisms, most obviously what is sometimes termed 'Western Marxism', but also the various kinds of post-structuralism which have in different ways emphasised the 'materiality of the sign'.

This question, that of the relation between Williams's cultural materialism and other, contemporaneous, would-be 'materialist' theories of culture, will be broached in chapter three, further explored in chapter four, and 'resolved', if only provisionally, in the concluding, fifth chapter. Chapter four takes as its theme the various disciplinary, or at least proto-disciplinary, forms of intellectual inquiry that have been significantly influenced either by Williams himself, by more generally cultural materialist notions, or, more commonly, by a combination of each. These matters are discussed in chapter four essentially in relation to the relatively small world of British intellectual life, and its various Anglophonic extensions overseas, most obviously here in Australia. In chapter five, however, we proceed to a necessarily tentative, though by no means entirely provisional, comparison between British cultural materialism and those developments in recent French and German thought most commonly canvassed as its rough equivalent, in particular the post-structuralist 'genealogy' of Michel Foucault, the cultural sociology of Pierre Bourdieu, and Jürgen Habermas's theory of communicative action. This last chapter, as also the book itself, finally concludes with a discussion of the respective relevance of these various theoretical humanisms and anti-humanisms, not only to the would-be academic discipline of cultural studies, but also to the wider prospects for a more general, emancipatory politics.

2

Culturalism

Much of the theoretical literature in cultural studies has revolved around a recurrent contrast between 'culturalism' and 'structuralism' (Johnson, 1979; Dermody et al., 1982), in which the former is typically represented by Williams, and perhaps by E. P. Thompson, the latter by an entire intellectual tradition reaching back from Lévi-Strauss and Barthes to Durkheim and Saussure. And if some have more recently sought to 'consign the culturalism-structuralist split to the past' (Turner, 1990:72; Bennett, 1986:xii–xvi), they have nonetheless done so in terms which radically privilege the latter. By way of correction, we might well begin by noting that there is, in fact, a similarly longstanding culturalist tradition behind Williams, one which reaches back at least to Burke and Cobbett, and one which Williams himself sought to map out in *Culture and Society*, and by entertaining the possibility, at least, that this culturalist legacy might have some continuing relevance to contemporary cultural studies. I use the term 'culturalism' here to denote, then, this mainly English tradition of essentially 'literary' speculation about the relationship between culture and society, in which the claims of culture, understood both as art and as 'way of life', are counterposed, normally antithetically, to those of an industrialised or industrialising, 'mechanical' or materialist civilisation. This is a tradition which in the late nineteenth and early twentieth centuries became institutionally organised, both in Britain and in Australia, into the academic discipline we now know as 'English'. Perhaps its most extreme formulation is to be found in F. R. Leavis himself, in the journal *Scrutiny* which he founded, and more generally in the 'Leavisism' of his close collaborators, most obviously Q. D. Leavis, but also, for example, Denys Thompson, and L. C. Knights. Certainly, it was Leavisism which was to provide Williams with his initial theoretical starting point. As he would later recall of the journal *Politics and Letters*, which he established and co-edited at Cambridge during 1947 and 1948:

> Our intention was to produce a review that would . . . unite radical left politics with Leavisite literary criticism . . . The immense attraction of Leavis lay in his cultural radicalism . . . It was the range of Leavis's attacks on academicism, on Bloomsbury, on metropolitan literary culture, on the commercial press, on advertising, that first took me. (Williams, 1979a:65–6)

What, then, was Leavisism?

Mass Civilisation and Minority Culture: Leavisite Idealism

It is characteristic of Leavis that he should have attempted no formal statement of the principles by which his literary and cultural criticism is guided. The nearest to such a formulation is in the essay 'Literary Criticism and Philosophy', written in reply to a challenge to defend his position 'more abstractedly' from the philosopher René Wellek. 'Your insistence on a firm grasp of the actual', Wellek had charged, 'presupposes you in the direction of a realist philosophy' (Wellek, 1937:376). Leavis's response was to counterpose the poet's concern with the 'concrete' to the philosopher's with the 'abstract'. 'The critic's aim', explained Leavis, 'is, first, to realize as sensitively and completely as possible this or that which claims his attention'; and then to situate the work under consideration into a hierarchy of judgement, by reference to other similar such works, that is, to 'an organization of similarly "placed" things, things that have found their bearings with regard to one another, and not a theoretical system determined by abstract considerations' (Leavis, 1962a:213). Leavis's resistance to explicit theorisation finds ultimate expression, therefore, in the famous dictum that 'My whole effort was to work in terms of concrete judgements and particular analyses: "This—doesn't it?—bears such a relation to that; this kind of thing—don't you find it so?—wears better than that?'" (ibid.:215).

This insistence on the concrete analysis of specific literary texts has all the appearance of traditional English empiricism. But appearances can be deceptive. Leavis's 'This is so, is it not?' formula avoids an explicit statement of evaluative criteria only because it assumes the existence of values already common both to the literary critic and to his or her readers: the values are unstated but present nonetheless. And these specifically literary values in turn form part of a wider system of cultural, social and historical evaluation. Let me call attention here to what seem five especially salient features of this Leavisite system: its organicist aesthetic; its anit-utilitarian social criticism; its pessimistic, even apocalyptic, historicism; its character-istically militant sense of the social role of the intellectual; and its cultural nationalism.

That Leavis's aesthetic represented a variant of organicism, structurally analogous not only to the cultural criticism of Matthew Arnold and T. S. Eliot but also to the great systems of classical German idealist philosophy, has become something of an intellec-tual commonplace. Leavis's organicism is most readily apparent in his sense of a literature as 'essentially something more than an accumulation of separate works: it has an organic form, or consti-tutes an organic order in relation to which the individual writer has . . . significance and . . . being' (ibid.184). The centre of Leavis's intellectual effort consists, then, in an attempt to map out the tradition of the English novel on the one hand, the tradition of English poetry on the other, each imagined in exactly such organicist terms. Conceived thus, the literary tradition is not simply an artefact of the critical enterprise, but rather an objective 'fact' of cultural history itself. It follows, then, that for Leavis writing which sits uncomfortably with 'the tradition' is not properly 'literature' at all: the obvious instances here include both popular fiction and the contemporary *avant-garde*. Leavis's organicism is operative both at the level of the cultural tradition as a whole and at that of the individual literary work. At this second level, it finds expression in the aesthetic ideal of an organic unity of form and content. This notion informs the invidious comparison between Lawrence and

Joyce, for example, by which the latter is judged inferior on the grounds that 'there is no organic principle determining, informing, and controlling [the work] into a vital whole' (Leavis, 1962b:36). Perhaps the point is made most explicitly, however, when Leavis identifies the central weakness of Flaubert's *Madame Bovary* as 'the discrepancy between the technical ("aesthetic") intensity, with the implied attribute of interest to the subject, and the actual moral and human paucity of this subject' (ibid.:22).

What must also be emphasised, however, is the way in which the organic properties of 'great' literature derive, in Leavis's view, from the organicism of human social life, at least in its 'normal', 'healthy' forms. Thus the central category of Leavis's aesthetic, hinted at in Wellek's charge of a tendency towards realism, is that of a commitment to 'life' itself as a value. For Leavis, great literature is that which can render a form adequate to the expression of life: 'the major novelists . . . count in the same ways as the major poets, in the sense that they are significant in terms of that human awareness they promote; awareness of the possibilities of life' (ibid.:10). Leavis was vehemently opposed to aestheticism, in the sense of *l'art pour l'art*. For him, the defining characteristic of the great English novelists is that 'they are all distinguished by a vital capacity for experience, a kind of reverent openness before life, and a marked moral intensity' (ibid.:17). Joseph Conrad, for example, is in Leavis's view 'one of those creative geniuses whose distinction is manifested in their being peculiarly alive in their time—peculiarly alive *to* it' (ibid.:32). Leavis's assessment of English poetry runs along similar lines, so that the central weakness of the nineteenth century is its other-worldliness, its flight from reality, and, correspondingly, Eliot's significance is in his ability to 'invent techniques . . . adequate to the ways of feeling, or modes of experience, of adult, sensitive moderns' (Leavis, 1938:25).

'Life', in Leavis's sense of the word, is by no means identical with reality, but rather a value to be set against many aspects of the real. Perhaps the most precise statement of what Leavis means by the term is to be found in his commentary on Blake that 'To be spontaneous, and in its spontaneity creative, is of the essence of life, which manifests itself in newness that can't be exhaustively reduced to the determined' (Leavis, 1972a:15). Such non-determined, spontaneous creativity remains for Leavis profoundly antithetical to a contemporary civilisation he judged irredeemably utilitarian in character. So understood, that is, as a 'canon' of 'great works', the literary tradition came to provide the comparatively new academic discipline of 'English Literature' with its central subject matter. By excluding the merely 'fictional', and much else besides, Leavis's aesthetic enabled a relatively precise definition and demarcation of the subject's intellectual and institutional boundaries.

Turning to those of his writings which might better be described as 'social criticism', here too we find the category of 'life' at the core of Leavis's critical apparatus. Leavis identifies the dominant values of modern British society as essentially utilitarian, or in his own memorable phrase, 'technologico-Benthamite', and deems them essentially hostile to life. In contemporary society, Leavis comments, 'there is a dawning unselfrecognised conviction that we can get on, and get on better, without much life' (ibid.:33). The cultural logic of such a civilisation, he argues, is one which militates against life, in so far as it is essentially materialistic, and thereby reduces all problems of value to the level of crude material acquisition. In a highly public response to C. P. Snow's 1959 Rede Lecture, Leavis described Snow as wholly representative of a world 'in which the vital inspiration, the creative drive, is "Jam tomorrow" (if you haven't any today) or (if you have it today) "More jam tomorrow"' (Leavis, 1962c:25). A materialism such as this, which Leavis views as chronically incapable of satisfying real human needs, is in his view by no means a 'merely' 'ideological' phenomenon. Quite the contrary: it arises as a direct consequence of the process of technological change precipitated by the industrial revolution. 'Technological change has marked cultural consequences', writes Leavis: 'There is an implicit logic that will impose, if not met by creative intelligence and corrective purpose, simplifying and reductive criteria of human need and human good, and generate, to form the mind and the spirit of civilization, disastrously false and inadequate conceptions of . . . ends'. (Leavis, 1972a:94–5) Thus, the material process of mass-production has two main cultural consequences, 'levelling-down' and 'standardization', each of which is seen as essentially inimical to life. Technological change is, for Leavis, destructive of both individuality and creativity, and tends toward the reduction of all human beings to the status of passive respondents to external material forces. Technologico-Benthamite civilisation is thus increasingly inhabited by 'the worker whose routine work, requiring or permitting no creative effort on his part, and no large active interest—little more, in fact than automatisms—leaves him incapable of any but the passive and the crude' (ibid.:87).

Given Leavis's assumptions as to the relationship between art and life, it follows that a society such as this must be of necessity hostile to art. Leavis is particularly gloomy about the prospects for poetry in the modern world:

> the finer values are ceasing to be a matter of even conventional concern for any except the minority capable of the highest level. Everywhere below, a process of standardization, mass-production, and levelling-down goes forward, and civilization is coming to mean a solidarity achieved by the exploitation of the most readily released response. So that poetry, in the future, if there is poetry, seems likely to matter even less to the world. (Leavis, 1938:213–14)

But poetry is only the extreme case of a more general problem. In fact, the whole of literature, of art, of humane culture, is threatened by the material dynamics of contemporary society. As Leavis himself would recall of the group involved in producing *Scrutiny* : 'The dialectic against which we had to vindicate literature and humane culture was that of the external or material civilization we lived in' (Leavis, 1963:5). That dialectic found its clearest impress in popular fiction on the one hand, commercial advertising on the other. Q. D. Leavis elaborated upon the culturally deleterious consequences of the former in her influential *Fiction and the Reading Public* :

> This for the sensitive minority is no laughing matter: these novelists are read by the governing classes as well as by the masses, and they impinge directly on the minority, menacing the standards by which they live . . . These writers . . . work upon and solidify herd prejudice and . . . debase the emotional currency by touching grossly on fine issues. (Leavis, 1979:65).

F. R. Leavis and Denys Thompson devoted much of their attention to the latter in their *Culture and Environment* (Leavis and Thompson,

1960), a manual for English teachers designed in part to educate their pupils in effective resistance to advertising. At times, Leavis's anti-utilitarianism runs strangely parallel to certain kinds of culturalist Marxism, most obviously that of the Frankfurt School. But the Leavisites themselves clearly understood Marxism in much the same fashion as did Parsons, that is, as in essence merely a sub-variant of utilitarianism. And if utilitarian capitalist civilisation was already materialist, then it followed, for Leavis, that Communist materialism would prove not so much a solution to as an exacerbation of that civilisation's most fundamental problems: 'to aim at solving the problems of civilization in terms of the "class war" is to aim . . . at completing the work of capitalism and its products' (Leavis, 1933:172).

The tone of almost unremitting pessimism which pervades much of Leavis's social criticism arises very clearly from his own peculiar interpretation of English history. For the Leavisites, the previous three hundred years could best be characterised as a process of disintegration and decline. Leavis himself drew heavily on George Sturt's *The Wheelwright's Shop*, both in *Culture and Environment* and in the later *Nor Shall My Sword*. In the former, for example, he describes the pre-industrial 'organic community' thus:

> Sturt's villagers expressed their human nature, they satisfied their human needs, in terms of the natural environment; and the things they made . . . together with their relations with one another constituted a human environment, and a subtlety of adjustment and adaptation, as right and inevitable. (Leavis and Thompson, 1960:91)

Such a community would remain as the implicit ideal, by comparison with which contemporary society would be judged and found wanting. The destruction of the old organic community and its replacement by a more recent, and inorganic, industrial civilisation becomes one of Leavis's central preoccupations: 'Its destruction . . . is the most important fact of recent history' (ibid.:87). And Leavis has little doubt as to the adverse consequences of this 'vast and terrifying disintegration' (ibid.). To Snow's account of the industrial revolution as essentially benign, Leavis would reply that: 'This, of course, is mere brute assertion, callous in its irresponsibility

. . . the actual history has been . . . incomparably and poignantly more complex than that' (Leavis, 1962c:24). The breakdown of the organic community produced, according to Leavis, a rupture between sophisticated and popular cultures. In Shakespeare or Marvell or Bunyan we can find clear evidence of a cultural unity between the sophisticated and the popular, such that, for example, 'Bunyan shows how the popular culture to which he bears witness could merge with literary culture at the level of great literature' (Leavis, 1962a:191). Such an achievement is possible, argues Leavis, because 'there is, behind the literature, a social culture and an art of living' (ibid.:190). But with the Augustans this unity disappears and 'sophisticated culture cuts itself off from the traditional culture of the people' (ibid.:192). The immediate consequence of industrialisation is the almost total elimination of the older popular culture: 'By Wordsworth's death, the Industrial Revolution had done its work and the traditional culture of the people was no longer there' (ibid.). In the longer term, sophisticated culture too would become, with the Victorians, increasingly obsessed with the construction of 'dream worlds' and correspondingly divorced from 'life'.

If this was history, then, as Leavis himself came to recognise, it was not history as conventionally understood by historians. Leavis's gloomy historicism, amounting in effect to a theory of cultural decline, ran directly contrary to much of the dominant historiographical wisdom. When Leavis sought to distance his work from the immediately cognate discipline of history, he did so on the grounds of the latter's positivist empiricism. This was not, as it is sometimes represented, a matter of Leavis's stress on the 'internal' analysis of the literary text, as opposed to the 'external' analysis of the text's historical context. Much more importantly, what was at stake here was the centrality of evaluation, both as applied to the text and as applied elsewhere. As becomes clear, for example, from Leavis's criticisms of the historian G. M. Trevelyan, questions of value pertain as much to historical context as to literary text. The unanswered, because unasked, questions in Trevelyan, Leavis insists, are:

> What, as a civilization to live in and be of, did England offer at such and such a time? As we pass from now to then, what light

is thrown on human possibilities—on the potentialities of civilized life? In what respects might it have been better to live then than now? What tentative conception of an ideal civilization are we prompted towards by the hints we gather from history?. (ibid.:200)

It is this sense of history (and sociology) as inadequately concerned with problems of value which leads Leavisism to its own peculiarly militant sense of the social role of the intellectual, and of the special nature of English studies in relation to that role. For Leavis, English was to be not merely one discipline among many but rather a rallying point for the defence of humane values in general against the depradations of utilitarian civilisation. Central to Leavis's own programme of action was the role of the ideal university English School, outlined in his *Education and the University* The implicit logic of technological change can be reversed, we have seen, if met by 'creative intelligence' and 'corrective purpose'. And the primary source of such an effort was to be located in the university English School. The 'literary mind', Leavis argued, is the central kind of mind: 'an intelligence with the sensitiveness, the flexibility and the disciplined mature preoccupation with value that should be the product of literary training' (Leavis, 1948:55). As such, there is nothing merely 'literary' about the literary mind: Leavis's model English School would aspire to assess the cultural value of whole communities, whole civilisations. Though Leavis recognised this would entail that 'everyone would have been required to come to fairly close terms . . . with other fields of special study' (ibid.:57), the central informing virtues would nonetheless be those of the literary mind. 'In any period', wrote Leavis, 'it is upon a very small minority that the discerning appreciation of art and literature depends'. This minority 'constitute the consciousness of the race (or a branch of it) at a given time. For such capacity does not belong merely to an aesthetic realm: it implies responsiveness to theory as well as to art, to science and philosophy in so far as these may affect the sense of the human situation and the nature of life' (ibid.:143–4). 'English' thus ceases to be a specialist discipline and becomes, in effect, the consciousness of the race. Such grand claims led Leavis by an almost inescapable logic to the view, aired in the polemic against Snow, that the English School would 'generate in the university a centre of consciousness (and conscience) for our civilization' (Leavis, 1962c:30). The fundamental radicalism of the Leavisite project inhered, then, in this rejectionist stance toward the already established intellectual culture, here represented by the hapless C. P. Snow. As Francis Mulhern has observed, Leavisism aspired to create 'an intellectual formation of a type virtually unknown in and deeply alien to English bourgeois culture: an "intelligentsia" in the classic sense of the term, a body of intellectuals dissociated from every established social interest' (Mulhern, 1981:326).

For all its distinctly un-English intellectual sectarianism, Leavisism also came to embody a form of often quite virulent English cultural nationalism. For much of its history, English studies has been justified on nationalist grounds: the 1921 Newbolt Report on the teaching of English, for example, recommended that the subject be established in the schools precisely as the centre of a national education in national consciousness (Baldick, 1983:95). Leavis's own insistence that the proper subject matter for the discipline was to be not cultural texts in general, not even 'literary' texts in general, but rather English literary texts in particular, betrays a similarly nationalist sensibility. When, during the 1960s, it was finally proposed to include foreign writers in a new Cambridge paper on the novel, Leavis was to argue that the study of Proust and Kafka 'would be a misdirection. There is nothing relevant there' (Williams, 1984a:17). This Leavisite nationalism is crucially evident, however, in Leavis's theory of language, in his improbable affirmation of the non-arbitrary nature of the English sign. For Leavis, it is in language itself, in its most literary moments of articulation, that the truths of a particular culture are most clearly formed. The essential value of a culture, Leavis argues, devolves upon its capacity to sustain a culturally superior minority: 'In their keeping . . . is the language, the changing idiom, upon which fine living depends, and without which distinction of spirit is thwarted and incoherent. By "culture" I mean the use of such a language' (Leavis, 1948:145). Hence the peculiar significance for Leavis of the literary culture within the wider general culture. And, in Leavis's view, English itself, in its 'Shakespearean use', is a language unlike either Latin or Greek in which 'words seem to do what they say' (Leavis, 1972b:58). It was this view which formed Leavis's famous dismissal of Milton: 'He exhibits a feeling *for* words rather than a capacity for feeling *through* words' (ibid.:53). Milton's use of English is so consistently remote from the spoken language, argues Leavis, that even 'habituation could not sensitize a medium so cut off from speech— speech that belongs to the emotional and sensory texture of actual living and is in resonance with the nervous system' (ibid.:54). The particular judgement on Milton is actually less significant here than the more general conception of the English language. For if the language is indeed thus, then the subject matter of literary studies must needs be constituted out of the Englishness of the language itself. Furthermore, the Englishness of the language is in turn an expression of the Englishness of the people and of their erstwhile common culture. The result is a nationalistic preoccupation with the superior virtues, if not exactly of the contemporary English, then of their peasant ancestors and of the legacy of the pre-industrial organic community bequeathed to the language by those ancestors.

Base and Superstructure: Communist Materialism

During the 1930s, almost exactly contemporaneously with the early development of the *Scrutiny* group, Marxism, or at least a certain account of it, came to exercise a considerable albeit temporary influence over significant sections of the British intelligentsia. This new Communist Marxism was especially influential among the natural scientists on the one hand, writers and literary critics on the other. The latter group included, for example, C. Day Lewis, W. H. Auden, Stephen Spender, Christopher Caudwell, Edward Upward, Ralph Fox and Alick West. Indeed, Leavis was clear that *Scrutiny* had developed in part by way of response to the Marxist challenge: 'We were anti-Marxist—necessarily so . . . intelligent, that is, a real interest in literature implied a conception of it very different from any that a Marxist could expound and explain . . . Marxist fashion gave us the doctrinal challenge' (Leavis, 1963:4). Williams himself was a member of the Communist Party from 1939 to 1941, during his first years as a student at Cambridge, despite subscribing to what he would later remember as 'a cultural stance in opposition to . . . "party attitudes" to literature—which we criticized as narrow and stuffy' (Williams, 1979a:46). For Williams, the appeal of Communist Marxism remained political rather than literary, and was in any case essentially short-lived. By the late 1940s, Williams and his collaborators on the journal *Politics and Letters* 'were convinced that we were the most radical element in the culture . . . we regarded the Communist Party as irrelevant because of the intellectual errors it had made' (ibid.:66). Williams would never resume his membership of the Communist Party. But his interest in, and relation to, Marxism as an intellectual system was to prove much more enduring. What kind of Marxism was it, then, which Williams first encountered through the British Communist Party?

Communist Marxism had inherited the base/superstructure formula from Marx and a strong preference for literary 'realism' from Engels. To these, it added an immediate diagnosis of contemporary capitalist society as crisis-ridden and of contemporary bourgeois culture as decadent. And, in the specific case of British Communist Marxism, all of this was compounded by a quasi-Romantic sense of the social mission of the creative writer. As we noted in chapter one, Marx's own Marxism had reserved the term 'superstructure' for the politico-legal order, as distinct from the cultural. Moreover, Marx's own formulation is distinctly cautious: 'the forms of social consciousness', he wrote, 'correspond' to 'the economic structure of society'; the 'mode of production', he continued, 'conditions' the 'general process of . . . intellectual life'; and, while 'economic conditions' can be 'determined with . . . precision', this is not the case for the 'ideological forms' (Marx, 1975:425–6). No doubt the central analogy with construction (foundation/superstructure) and the powerfully evocative reference to the precision of natural science do indeed combine to suggest a process of mechanical causation, where the economy is the cause and culture the effect. Much of that suggestion is nonetheless belied by the carefully qualifying verbs, 'correspond' and 'conditions', rather than 'causes'. But whatever Marx's own intentions, Communist Marxism very clearly adhered to a strongly deterministic version of the base/superstructure model. Neither Marx nor Engels ever actually elaborated any kind of prescriptive theory of aesthetics, and both appear to have enjoyed fairly catholic literary tastes. There are, however, very many references to literary matters scattered throughout both their published and unpublished writings. And Engels, in particular, engaged in a series of private 'literary' correspondences in which he employed the category of 'realism' as an informal criterion of aesthetic value. In a letter to Margaret Harkness in April 1888, for example, he wrote: 'Realism, to my mind, employs, besides truth of detail, the truthful reproduction of typical characters under typical circumstances' (Marx and Engels, 1947:41). Here and in other letters to Minna Kautsky and Lassalle (ibid.:40–63), Engels in effect appeals to a set of fairly conventional notions, then current, about realism so as to make immediate, and in truth fairly casual, judgements on contemporary writing. But whatever Engels's own intentions, or lack thereof, his remarks were taken up by Communist Marxism as the basis for much more generally prescriptive theories of literary value.

A key influence on the formation of Communist theories of culture, though not himself a Communist, was the Russian Marxist writer Georgei Plekhanov. In *The Development of the Monist View of History*, first published in 1895, Plekhanov had viewed culture as the complex product of an interaction between psychology and economy, in which the latter plays the determining role, the former the adaptive: 'Psychology adapts itself to economy. But this adaptation is a complex process . . . on the one hand the "iron laws" of movement of the "string" . . . on the other . . . on the "string" . . . there grows up the *"garment of Life" of ideology'* (Plekhanov, 1956:265). In *Art and Social Life,* published in 1912, he sought to understand art as the twin product of biology on the one hand, material history on the other. Thus: 'The ideal of beauty that obtains at a given time . . . has its roots partly in the biological conditions of development of the human species . . . partly in the historical conditions in which this society . . . arose and existed' (Plekhanov, 1978:23). Plekhanov conceives this material history, however, as operating in a very peculiar fashion, as imposing itself directly upon the art work via the medium of the work's own artistic content. Content is thus equated with the realistic representation of material history, not in the sense of a particular set of cultural conventions designed to create the illusion of an accurate depiction of some extra-textual reality, but rather that of a genuinely accurate depiction of a genuinely extra-textual reality. Artistic form thereby becomes a superstructure, the material base of which is artistic content, understood as somehow coextensive with historical reality itself: 'the value of a work of art is determined, in the last analysis by its content' (ibid.:19–20). And so artistic realism comes to constitute the measure of literary value: 'when a work distorts reality, it is a failure' (ibid.:63). What in Engels had amounted to little more than conventionally informed personal preference is here transformed into a prescriptive aesthetic. For Plekhanov, the 'allegedly artistic exercises' of bourgeois modernisms such as Cubism are the product of 'individualism in the period of bourgeois decay', an individualism which condemns the artist 'to barren preoccupation with his own private and empty experiences and sickly, fantastic inventions' (ibid.:53–5). All three themes, the determining base and determined superstructure, artistic realism as a valorised mode of cognition, and the decadence of non-realistic bourgeois art forms, were to be taken up and elaborated upon by the 1934 Soviet Writers' Congress, at which the new Communist cultural policies of 'socialist realism' and 'revolutionary romanticism' were first announced.

In his opening speech to the Writers' Congress, Andrey Zhdanov, then Secretary of the Central Committee of the Soviet Communist Party, counterposed Soviet socialist realism to bourgeois literary decadence in terms clearly reminiscent of Plekhanov. The success of Soviet literature, Zhdanov observes, 'is an expression of the successes . . . of our socialist system' (Zhdanov, 1977:17). For Zhdanov as for Plekhanov, under 'socialism' as much as under capitalism, great art serves to 'express' social reality. And for Zhdanov as for Plekhanov, the greatness of great art consists precisely in this indebtedness to reality: 'Our Soviet writer', he explains, 'derives the material of his works of art . . . from the life and experience of the men and women of Dnieprostroy, of Magnitostry' (Zhdanov, 1977:20). To achieve this 'means knowing life so as to be able to depict it truthfully', he continues, 'not simply as "objective reality", but to depict reality in its revolutionary development' (ibid.:21). By contrast:

> The present state of bourgeois literature is such that it is no longer able to create great works of art . . . Everything now is growing

stunted—themes, talents, authors, heroes . . . Characteristic of the decadence and decay of bourgeois culture are the orgies of mysticism and superstition, the passion for pornography, (ibid.:19).

Later in the Congress, Karl Radek would proceed along similar lines: from the general proposition that 'literature is a reflection of social life' (Radek, 1977:74); to an intemperate denunciation of Joyce's *Ulysses* as a 'heap of dung, crawling with worms, photographed by a cinema apparatus through a microscope' (ibid.:153); to a celebration of realism as 'reflecting reality as it is, in all its complexity, in all its contrariety, and not only capitalist reality, but also that other, new reality—the reality of socialism' (ibid.:156–7). The precise extent to which Soviet Communist leaders believed their own rhetoric remains a decidedly moot point. Certainly, a truly realistic account of 'the reality of socialism', such as Solzhenitsyn would eventually produce in *One Day in the Life of Ivan Denisovich, Cancer Ward* and *The First Circle*, would have earned its 1934 author a prominent part in the Show Trials of the late 1930s. Indeed, even as it was, that fate befell many of the Congress participants, not least Nikolai Bukharin, whose contribution on poetry and poetics figures prominently in the 1935 English language edition of the main Congress speeches. Assuming their subjective sincerity, however, one is still struck by the apparent contradiction between a pseudo-deterministic sociology, which insists that the base determines the superstructure, and a voluntarist prescriptive aesthetic, which insists that it should do so. Were the sociology to prove valid, then one cannot but reflect that the aesthetic would thereby be rendered very nearly redundant.

Very nearly, but not entirely so. In Soviet Communism itself, sociology and aesthetic were reconciled by virtue of the Communist Party's self-proclaimed role as 'the midwife of history'. And in so far as art and literature were concerned, it was not so much 'socialist realism' as 'revolutionary romanticism' which served to denote the proper function of the cultural midwife. Following Stalin, Zhdanov had preferred to introduce this latter notion through the metaphor of the engineer rather than that of the midwife:

To be an engineer of human souls means standing with both feet firmly planted on the basis of real life. And this in its turn denotes a rupture with romanticism of the old type, which depicted a non-existent life and non-existent heroes . . . Our literature . . . must be a romanticism of a new type, revolutionary romanticism . . . Soviet literature should be able to portray our heroes; it should be able to glimpse our tomorrow. This will be no utopian dream, for our tomorrow is already being prepared for today by dint of conscious planned work. (Zhdanov, 1977:21–2)

In the most literal of senses, then, Zhdanov envisages the role of the writer as that of social engineer. What both the Soviet authorities in general and Zhdanov in particular were increasingly to demand, and imperatively so, was an art that would be of directly political use to the new Soviet state. As the exiled Trotsky would dismissively argue: 'The official art of the Soviet Union—and there is no other over there—resembles totalitarian justice, that is to say, it is based on lies and deceit' (Trotsky, 1970:106).

But even at the Writers' Congress itself, a second and rather more defensible version of revolutionary romanticism had been suggested by Bukharin. 'Socialist realism dares to "dream"', Bukharin proposes:

If socialist realism is distinguished by its active, operative character; if it does not give just a dry photograph of a process; if it projects the entire world of passion and struggle into the future; if it raises the heroic principle to the throne of history— then revolutionary romanticism is a component part of it . . . In our circumstances romanticism is connected above all with heroic themes; its eyes are turned, not on the heaven of metaphysics, but on the earth, in all its senses—on triumph over the enemy and triumph over nature. (Bukharin, 1977:253–4)

It is the future as freely chosen, heroic aspiration, rather than as obligatory policy objective, with which Bukharin hopes to inspire such revolutionary romanticisms. Though Bukharin himself would never have countenanced the thought, this is not really so very far from Blake or Shelley. And while Bukharin's imminent disgrace would render him a non-person, whose ideas could be cited by Communists only as objects of disavowal, it was nonetheless to be this much more properly Romantic version of revolutionary romanticism that would resonate the more powerfully within the ranks of the British Communist Party. Interestingly, Christopher Caudwell's highly regarded *Illusion and Reality* was to include in its bibliography entries for Bukharin and Plekhanov, but for neither Zhdanov nor Radek (Caudwell, 1946:300, 308).

Caudwell was, in fact, by far the most influential of the British Communist cultural theorists. Williams himself remembers Ralph Fox's *The Novel and the People* as the more 'central work' and doubts that he came across Caudwell's writing during his time in the Communist Party (Williams, 1979a:44). It was Caudwell's influence, nonetheless, which was to prove the more enduring, so much so that in 1958 Williams would single him out as 'the best-known of these English Marxist critics' (Williams, 1963:268). *Illusion and Reality* was first published in 1937, only a few months after Caudwell had been killed in action with the International Brigade; it was republished in a new edition in 1946, and reprinted again in 1947, 1950, 1955, 1958 and 1966. *The Novel and the People* was also first published in 1937, again only months after its own author's death in Spain; it was reprinted twice, in 1944 and 1948, and remained out of print thereafter until 1979.

For Caudwell, as for Communist Marxism generally, the literary superstructures remained essentially an effect of the developing material base. 'What is the basis of literary art?' he wrote, 'What is the inner contradiction which produces its own onward movement? Evidently it can only be a special form of the contradiction which produces the whole movement of society' (Caudwell, 1946:201). This contradiction, he proceeds to elaborate, is that of 'the endless struggle between man and Nature' (ibid.), a struggle which Caudwell himself defines simply as 'life', but which is in fact much closer to what Marx meant by the term 'mode of production'. Literature is thus essentially a by-product of economic activity: 'Poetry is clotted social history, the emotional sweat of man's struggle with Nature' (ibid.:130). In his opening, quasi-anthropological account of the historical origins of poetry, Caudwell writes that 'the developing complex of society, in its struggle with the environment, secretes poetry as it secretes the technique of the harvest, as part of its non-biological and specifically human adaptation to existence' (ibid.:29–30). Caudwell's historical sociology defines poetry in effect as an 'expression' of one or another stage in the development of the mode of production. Cultural modernity is thus 'the superstructure of the bourgeois revolution in production', and modern poetry notoriously *'capitalist* poetry' (ibid.:55). In his historical survey of the development of modern English poetry, Caudwell sets out to establish strict correlations between specific periods in the development of capitalist society, the general characteristics of the equivalent literary-historical periods, and the technical characteristics of the corresponding poetic forms. The historical periodisation is precisely specified: 'Primitive Accumulation' runs from 1550 to 1600; 'The Industrial Revolution and the "Anti-Jacobin" Reaction' from 1750 to 1825; 'The Epoch of Imperialism' from 1900 to 1930. According to Caudwell, each of these (and there are nine in all) gives rise to certain quite specific general and technical characteristics in poetry. During the period of 'Primitive Accumulation', for instance, the general characteristic is that of the 'dynamic force of individuality', the technical characteristics lyrics suitable for group singing on the one hand, and iambic rhythm on the other. 'The iambic rhythm', writes Caudwell, 'is allowed to flower luxuriantly and naturally; it indicates the free and boundless development of the personal will' (ibid.:117).

Like Plekhanov, Caudwell thinks of culture as having an essentially adaptive function: 'The poem adapts the heart to a new purpose, without changing the eternal desires of men's hearts' (ibid.:30). In Caudwell's view, these eternal desires are fixed by the human 'genotype', that is, 'the more or less common set of instincts in each man' (ibid.:124). And for Caudwell, as for Plekhanov, a socio-functional explanation for the existence of art leads easily to a valorisation of realist cultural forms. Art, he writes, 'remoulds external reality nearer to the likeness of the genotype's instincts . . . Art becomes more socially and biologically valuable and greater art the more that remoulding is comprehensive and true to the nature of reality' (ibid.:261). During the 'Epoch of Imperialism', which in Caudwell's view had only recently come to an end, the central technical characteristic of bourgeois poetry had become the 'attempt entirely to separate the world of art from that of society', which culminated finally in the "completely free" word of *surréalisme'* (ibid.:121). Such art gives rise eventually to 'the spectacle of culture tragically perishing because its matrix, society, has become dispersed and sterile . . . the pathos of art . . . torn by insoluble conflicts and perplexed by all kinds of unreal phantasies' (ibid.:297). For Caudwell, 'The Final Capitalist Crisis', which he dates '1930–?', gives rise to the historically determined opportunity 'once again to give social value to all the technical resources, developed by the movement of the preceding stages' (ibid.:122). But, though the opportunity itself is historically determined, the capacity to avail oneself thereof remains both a matter of political choice and a matter for political struggle. Hence, Caudwell's concluding address to the bourgeois artist, made unselfconsciously in the name of 'the conscious proletariat':

> There is no neutral world of art, free from categories or determining causes. Art is a social activity . . . You must choose between class art which is unconscious of its causality and is therefore to that extent false and unfree, and proletarian art which is becoming conscious of its causality and will therefore emerge as the truly free art of communism . . . Our demand—that your art should be proletarian—is *not* a demand that you apply dogmatic categories and Marxist phrases to art . . . We ask that you should *really* live in the new world and not leave your soul behind in the past . . . We shall know that this transition has taken place when your art has become *living;* then it will be proletarian. Then we shall cease to criticise it for its deadness. (ibid.:288–9)

Doubtless there is much in Caudwell that is idiosyncratic, indeed original, his psychologism for instance. But both the general structure of Communist Marxism and the more specifically Romantic, as distinct from utilitarian, Bukharinite as distinct from Zhdanovite, conception of the role of the militant artist-intellectual recur throughout the British Communist cultural criticism of the 1930s. Alick West, for example, could move readily from the quasi-sociological proposition that the 'source of value in the work of literature is . . . social energy and activity' (West, 1975:99), to the quasi-Romantic prescription that 'the criticism of our lives, by the test of whether we are helping to forward the most creative movement in our society, is the only effective foundation of the criticism of literature' (ibid.:102). This most creative movement, West spells out, 'is socialism', the function of criticism, therefore, 'to judge literature, both content and form, as a part of this movement' (ibid.:102–3). And criticism 'can only fulfil this function', he adds, 'if it takes part in this movement on the side of the workers of the world' (ibid.). A similarly quasi-sociological moment informs Ralph Fox's understanding of the role of the writer as that of 'winning the knowledge of truth, of reality' (Fox, 1979:37). Art, he continues, is a 'means by which man grapples with and assimilates reality' (ibid.). Such realism had been present in the early bourgeois novel, Fox explains, but in the twentieth century, in the age of 'philosophical decadence' and 'political counter-revolution', then 'no full and free expression of human personality is possible' (ibid.:96–7). What is possible, of course, is the 'new realism' that is socialist realism. Thence, once more, the quasi-Romantic call to arms: 'we must strain our inventive and creative faculties to the utmost . . . let us go into the fight together encouraged by the thought that the fate of our language and the struggles to develop it, have . . . always been . . . closely bound up with the struggles of our country for national salvation' (ibid.:138).

In each case, determinist sociology and Romantic polemic are held in dynamic tension only by a near-apocalyptic understanding of the supposed 'general crisis of capitalism', in many respects startlingly reminiscent of Leavis's own. For it was the very urgency of the perceived crisis, the same urgency that compelled both Caudwell and Fox to volunteer for Spain, which conjured up, as it were, the necessity of voluntarism. But when western capitalism settled into its long postwar boom, all of this began to seem hopelessly antiquated. As Williams himself was to recall:

> It may have seemed a natural response [to Leavisism] to retort that the point was not how to read a poem, but how to write one that meant something in the socio-political crisis of the time. But when the productive mood which was our way of replying by not replying faded away after the War, and we had to engage in literary criticism or history proper, we found we were left with nothing. (Williams, 1979:45)

Left Culturalism: A Provisional Synthesis

Left with nothing by Communist Marxism, but irreconcilably distanced from Leavisism by virtue of its seemingly endemic political conservatism and cultural elitism, the more independently minded left-wing British intellectuals of the 1950s slowly began to forge their own 'third way', both in practical politics and in cultural theory. The politics became that of the 'New left'; the theory what would be represented in structuralist retrospect as 'culturalism', but is perhaps more accurately described as 'left culturalism'. The founding moment of the British New Left, as a political movement, was constituted out of the double political crisis of 1956: on the one hand, the Anglo-French invasion of Egypt, and the crisis thereby occasioned within Britain itself; on the other, the Soviet invasion of Hungary, and the subsequent crisis within the international Communist movement, not least in the ranks of the Communist Party of Great Britain. The founding theoretical moment of left culturalism can be located more precisely in the early writings of three 'key' figures: Williams himself, the historian E. P. Thompson, and a second literary and cultural critic, Richard Hoggart. Both Williams and Hoggart were by origin working-class 'scholarship boys'; both Williams and Thompson were ex-Communists. All three had been trained as undergraduates in English Literature, Thompson and Williams at Cambridge, Hoggart at Leeds; all three had seen active service in the British Army during the Second World War; all three had worked in adult education, Thompson in the Extra-Mural Department at Leeds University, Hoggart in the Department of Adult Education at Hull, Williams in Extra-Mural Studies at Oxford. All three would come to occupy prominent positions in the intellectual landscape of the 1960s.

Much more so than Williams, it was Thompson who stood closest to the political centre of the movement of '1956', initially as the dissident Communist co-editor of the *Reasoner*, later the ex-Communist co-editor of the *New Reasoner,* and later still one of the founders of the *New Left Review*. Moreover, something at least of what would become 'left culturalism' had begun to be explored in the first edition of Thompson's *William Morris* (1955); rather more in the remarkable *New Reasoner* essay, 'Socialist Humanism' (1957); and eventually a great deal more in the magisterial *The Making of the English Working Class* (1963). *William Morris* had opened the way with its deeply appreciative study of a writer hitherto excluded from the canonical wisdom both of Leavisism and of official Communist Marxism. If Thompson here reclaimed Morris for

Marxism, then he also, and simultaneously, discovered in Morris much of the strength of the earlier Romantic critique of utilitarianism. As Thompson would later recall, 'the book . . . is, in a central respect, an argument about the Romantic tradition . . . Morris, by 1955, had claimed me. My book was then . . . already a work of muffled "revisionism"' (Thompson, 1977:769, 810). That revisionism became explicit during the often bitter controversies of the following years. These culminated in the famous essay on 'Socialist Humanism', in which Thompson quite deliberately set out to repudiate the base/superstructure formula as 'belittling . . . conscious human agency in the making of history'; and sought, equally deliberately, to explain the criminality of Stalinist politics as itself an effect of the economic determinism of official, orthodox Marxism.

The Making of the English Working Class built on this theoretical and political legacy, and on an extraordinary richness of empirical detail, so as to produce what Thompson himself would term 'a biography of the English working class from its adolescence until its early manhood' (Thompson, 1963:11). The base/superstructure model is here not so much discarded as transcended, or at least definitively outflanked, and on Communist Marxism's own preferred terrain, moreover, that of the working class and working-class consciousness, by a history of political struggle and popular culture, trade unionism and religion, community and conflict, in which class is understood as a cultural process as much as an economic phenomenon. The book's opening lines explain it to be 'a study in an active process, which owes as much to agency as to conditioning. The working class did not rise like the sun at an appointed time. It was present at its own making' (ibid.:9). The book is also, of course, a testament to the 'heroic culture' of a working class which 'nourished, for fifty years, and with incomparable fortitude, the Liberty Tree' (ibid.:832). That culture is, for Thompson, clearly something of very considerable value in itself. In the book's closing lines, Thompson also harks back to Morris, if only obliquely, when he draws attention to the element in common between this working-class resistance to utilitarianism which provides much of his subject matter, and that other tradition of Romantic anti-utilitarianism:

Such men met Utilitarianism in their daily lives, and they sought to throw it back not blindly, but with intelligence and moral passion . . . In these same years, the great Romantic criticism of Utilitarianism was running its parallel but altogether separate course. After William Blake, no mind was at home in both cultures, nor had the genius to interpret the two traditions to each other. In the failure of the two traditions to come to a point of junction, something was lost. How much we cannot be sure, for we are among the losers. (ibid.)

The theoretical moment of 1956 had registered much more visibly, however, in the work of dissident ex-Leavisites than in that of dissident ex-Communists. The key texts here are undoubtedly Hoggart's *The Uses of Literacy* (Hoggart, 1958), first published in 1957 by Leavis's own publisher, Chatto & Windus, and Williams's *Culture and Society,* published the following year, again by Chatto. It should come as little surprise, then, that a discussion between Williams and Hoggart, around the theme of working-class culture, should have figured in the first issue of the *New Left Review* (Hoggart and Williams, 1960). *The Uses of Literacy* was extremely well received: the paperback edition, first published in 1958, was reprinted in 1959, 1960, 1962, 1963, 1965, 1966, 1968 and 1969 (and many times thereafter, we might add). It marks the initial point at which post-Leavisite culturalism decisively shifts emphasis away from 'literature' and towards 'culture'. The book is divided into two parts, the first of which, 'An "Older" Order', provides what is in effect an ethnographic account of the North of England working-class culture within which Hoggart himself had been nurtured. This culture, that of the interwar years, is assessed positively, as is the extent to which some of its elements still persist. But Hoggart's central theme, outlined in the book's second part, 'Yielding Place to New', is that of the damage done the older culture by the newer mass arts, newspapers, books, magazines, and so on. Here, Hoggart makes use of the techniques of Leavisite practical criticism so as to analyse such popular texts. He summarises his own argument thus: 'The old forms of class culture are in danger of being replaced by a poorer kind of classless . . . culture . . . and this is to be regretted' (Hoggart, 1958:343). Like the Leavises, Hoggart was arguing a theory of cultural decline; like the Leavises, he attached major responsibility for this state of affairs to the commercial mass media. For Hoggart, however, it was the culture of the working class itself, rather than that of the 'sensitive minority', that needed to be valorised, if only so as, in turn, to be elegised. He remains particularly acute, moreover, on the ways in which 'competitive commerce' had been able to undermine the older order, precisely by manipulating that order's own resources against itself, thus learning 'to express our habitual moral assumptions but in such a way that they weaken the moral code they evoke; to say the right things for the wrong reasons' (ibid.:244).

Hoggart's achievement had been to divest Leavisism of something at least of its cultural elitism, if not perhaps of its nostalgia, Thompson's to divest Marxism of its economic determinism, and to make explicit what had previously only ever been an implicit, and barely acknowledged, Romanticism. But the achievement is in each case both reactive and contained: Hoggart reacts against, but nonetheless within, Leavisism; Thompson against, but nonetheless within, the then received version of Marxism. In Williams's *Culture and Society*, by contrast, as in *The Long Revolution,* first published in 1961 and 'planned and written as a continuation of the work begun in . . . *Culture and Society*' (Williams, 1965:9), we find something much closer to a proper synthesis between idealism and materialism, Leavisism and Communist Marxism. Williams inherited from Leavisism a commitment to holistic conceptions of culture and methods of analysis, a strong sense of the importance of the particular, whether in art or in 'life', and an insistence on the absolute centrality of culture. He rejected its cultural elitism, however, especially as displayed in the 'mass civilisation versus minority culture' topos. From Communist Marxism, he inherited a radically socialistic critique of the 'materiality' of ruling-class political, economic and cultural power, while rejecting the barely disguised economic determinism of the base/superstructure model.

The central procedure of *Culture and Society* could not be more Leavisite: to move, by way of close readings of a series of particular texts, to the account of a distinctively 'English' national 'tradition'. Furthermore, Williams's sense of the intellectual content of this tradition has much in common with that of Leavis or of Eliot. And for Williams, as for Leavis, the tradition is seen as developing in more or less explicit antagonism to utilitarianism (though this remains in many respects a surprisingly underdeveloped theme). Williams's strategic purpose was nonetheless radically opposed to the explicit cultural and political conservatism displayed by Eliot, and increasingly by the Leavises too. For Williams sought to demonstrate that, in its very complexity, the 'culture and society' tradition remained not only finally unassimilable to any obvious conservativism but also often openly amenable to radical, indeed socialistic, interpretation. This is not to suggest that Williams retained anything more than an entirely residual sympathy for Communist Marxism. The particular judgement on Caudwell, that 'for the most part his discussion is not even specific enough to be wrong' (Williams, 1963:268), as also the general conclusion on Marxism, that 'even if the economic element is determining, it determines a whole way of life, and it is to this, rather than to the economic system alone, that the literature has to be related' (ibid.:272), both attest to the very considerable distance that Williams had travelled since leaving the Communist Party. But, like Thompson, Williams nonetheless sees in Morris a 'pivotal figure' (ibid.:165), whose attempt to reconcile Romantic anti-utilitarianism and working-class opposition to capitalism suggest 'directions which . . . have become part of a general social movement' (ibid.). 'The significance of Morris in this tradition' he writes, 'is that he sought to attach its general values to an actual and growing social force: that of the organized working class. This was the most remarkable attempt that had so far been made to break the general deadlock' (ibid.:153). Like Thompson, Williams would himself aspire to renew that attempt in his own work.

Culture and Society is divided into three parts, dealing respectively with the years 1790 to 1870, 1870 to 1914, and 1914 to 1950. Williams summarises the general argument thus in the 'Conclusion':

> In the first period . . . we find the long effort to compose a general attitude towards the new forces of industrialism and democracy . . . in this period . . . the major opinions and descriptions emerge. Then . . . there is a breaking-down into narrower fronts, marked by a particular specialism in attitudes to art, and, in the general

field, by a preoccupation with direct politics. After 1914 these definitions continue, but there is a growing preoccupation, reaching a climax after 1945, with the issues raised not only by the inherited problems but by new problems arising from the development of mass media of communication and the general growth of large-scale organizations'. (ibid.:286–7)

Immediately thereafter, Williams proceeds to the 'personal conclusion' (ibid.:287) that is perhaps the most remarkable, and certainly at the time the most controversial, section in the book. Quite fundamentally, he begins by rejecting the Leavisite notion of 'mass civilization', and with it the notion of 'masses': 'There are in fact no masses; there are only ways of seeing people as masses' (ibid.:289). He rejects also the Leavisite notion of a distinctively valuable minority culture, but does so nonetheless in distinctly Leavisite terms. A culture, Williams writes, 'is not only a body of intellectual and imaginative work; it is also and essentially a whole way of life' (ibid.:311). In principle this is little different from Leavis's, or indeed Eliot's, sense of the connectedness of culture as art, and culture as way of life. But in the practical application of the principle, Williams so expands its range as to include within 'culture' the 'collective democratic institution', by which he means, primarily, the trade union, the co-operative, and the working-class political party (ibid.:313). As he would later write, 'culture is ordinary' (Williams, 1958).

Thus redefined, Eliot's and Leavis's notions of a single common culture become supplemented, and importantly qualified, by that of a plurality of class cultures. Yet despite such qualification, the normative ideal of a common culture remains central: 'We need a common culture, not for the sake of an abstraction, but because we shall not survive without it' (Williams, 1963:304). A common culture may not yet properly exist, but it remains desirable nonetheless, and moreover, it provides for Williams, as it had for Leavis, the essential theoretical ground from which to mount an organicist critique of utilitarian individualism. A common culture could never be properly such, Williams argues, if established on the basis of the kind of vicarious participation which Leavis and Eliot had sanctioned. 'The distinction of a culture in common', he writes in the book's closing pages, 'is that . . . selection is freely and commonly made and remade. The tending is a common process, based on a common decision' (ibid.:322). In a characteristically leftist move, Williams thus relocates the common culture from the idealised historical past it had occupied in Leavis to the not too distant, still to be made, democratically socialist future. And it is in the working-class 'idea of solidarity' that Williams finds 'potentially the real basis of a society' (ibid.:318).

If the common culture is not yet fully common, then it follows that the literary and cultural tradition should be seen not as the objective unfolding of the consciousness of a people, as the Leavisites had argued, but as the outcome, in part, of a set of interested selections made in the present: 'a tradition is always selective, and . . . there will always be a tendency for this process of selection to be related to and even governed by the interests of the class that is dominant' (ibid.:307–8). Where Leavis had revered a 'great tradition', Williams would thus discover a selective tradition. But, even as he insisted on the class determinations of culture, Williams was careful also to note the extent to which such distinctions of class are complicated, especially in the field of intellectual and imaginative work, by 'the common elements resting on a common language' (ibid.:311). For Williams, any direct reduction of art to class, such as had clearly been canvassed by Caudwell, remained entirely unacceptable. 'The area of culture', he observes, 'is usually proportionate to the area of a language rather than to the area of a class' (ibid.:307). This argument is repeated, and significantly elaborated upon, in the opening theoretical chapters of *The Long Revolution*:

> The selective tradition creates, at one level, a general human culture; at another level, the historical record of a particular society; at a third level . . . a rejection of considerable areas of what was once a living culture . . . selection will be governed by many kinds of special interest, including class interest . . . The traditional culture of a society will always tend to correspond to its *contemporary* system of interests and values. (Williams, 1965:68)

Once again, the stress falls on selection according to class-specific criteria, but once again, also, on the reality of a truly general human culture.

It is here, too, that Williams proposes an initial theorisation of the concept of 'structure of feeling', a term actually coined in the much earlier *Preface to Film* (Williams and Orrom, 1954), but not hitherto given any extensive theoretical articulation. 'In one sense', he writes, 'this structure of feeling is the culture of a period: it is the particular living result of all the elements in the general organization' (ibid.:64). He continues: 'in this respect . . . the arts of a period . . . are of major importance . . . here . . . the actual living sense, the deep community that makes the communication possible, is naturally drawn upon' (ibid.:64–5). A structure of feeling, Williams makes clear, is neither universal nor class-specific, though it is 'a very deep and wide possession' (ibid.:65). Nor is it formally learned, he speculates, and thence follows its often peculiarly generational character: 'the new generation will have its own structure of feeling, which will not appear to have come "from" anywhere' (ibid.). This concept of 'structure of feeling' was to prove quite extraordinarily fruitful. In *The English Novel*, for example, Williams would attempt to show how, from Dickens to Lawrence, the novel became one medium among many by which people sought to master and absorb new experience, through the articulation of a structure of feeling the key problem of which was that of the 'knowable community' (Williams, 1974a:14–15). In *Drama from Ibsen to Brecht*, he would produce an account of the development of naturalism and of expressionism in the modern theatre, which would be organised around precisely 'the history and significance of the main dramatic forms—the conventions and structures of feeling' (Williams, 1973a:14). The concept of structure of feeling would also occupy a commanding position in Williams's later cultural materialism.

In *The Long Revolution* itself, Williams sought to chart the long history of the emergence of modernity, and of the interrelationships, within British society, between the democratic revolution, the industrial revolution, and that 'cultural revolution' which became embodied in the extension and actual or potential democratisation of communications (Williams, 1965:10–12). As Williams himself later recalled, the book elicited an extremely hostile immediate response: 'There was a full-scale attack of the most bitter kind in certain key organs . . . *Culture and Society* soon acquired the reputation of being a decent and honourable sort of book, whereas this was a scandalous work. It was a standard complaint that I had been corrupted by sociology, that I had got into theory . . . it was perceived as a much more dangerous book' (Williams, 1979a:133–4). The central novelty of *The Long Revolution,* and the source of much of this hostility, actually lies in its form, in its peculiar combination of an extensive opening theoretical discussion, with an essentially 'sociological' substantive second part, and an expressly political third part. There is much that must have been offensively innovative in each. The opening theoretical discussions, in which the concept of structure of feeling is elaborated, are both dense and original. There was something distinctly un-English about this Welshman's theorising. The second part moves to supplement the more conventional procedures of Leavisite textual criticism with a much more material analysis of the historical development of a number of major British cultural institutions. There are pioneering analyses of the education system and the growth of the reading public, the popular press and the development of 'Standard English'; these are followed, in turn, by chapters on the social backgrounds of a selection of canonical English writers, on the social history of dramatic forms and on the contemporary novel, all of which remain disturbingly 'sociological' in their general import. The concluding third part, on 'Britain in the 1960s', in effect an exploratory inquiry into the structure of feeling of the early 1960s, critically addresses the politico-cultural problems of the apparent moral decline of the labour movement (ibid.:328–9). The combination of a sharply analytical intelligence and an at times near-utopian radical vision, which informs much of this last essay, must have spoken powerfully and provocatively to a society slowly shrugging off the moral and political conservatism of the 1950s.

What holds the three parts of the book together, however, is a very strong underlying sense of the materiality of culture, at once a restatement and a transcendence of the position originally outlined in *Culture and Society*. 'It was certainly an error', Williams wrote against Leavisite humanism, 'to suppose that values or art-works could be adequately studied without reference to the particular society within which they were expressed' (ibid.:61). But, 'it is equally an error', he wrote against Communist Marxism, 'to suppose that the social explanation is determining, or that the values and works are mere by-products' (ibid.). He moves thence to what might well be the book's central set of propositions:

> If the art is part of the society, there is no solid whole, outside it, to which . . . we concede priority. The art is there, as an activity, with the production, the trading, the politics, the raising of families . . . It is . . . not a question of relating the art to the society, but of studying all the activities and their interrelations, without any concession of priority to any one of them we may choose to abstract . . . I would define the theory of culture as the study of relationships between elements in a whole way of life. The analysis of culture is the attempt to discover the nature of the organization which is the complex of these relationships. Analysis of particular works or institutions is, in this context, analysis of their essential kind of organization, the relationships which works or institutions embody as parts of the organization of a whole. (ibid.:61–3)

Here, then, was the prospectus for what would soon become a thoroughgoing cultural materialism.

3

Cultural Materialism

I n the interim between the first publication of *The Long Revolution* in 1961 and that of *Marxism and Literature* in 1977, Williams's work was to proceed by way of a series of often radically innovative encounters with an extremely diverse set of substantive issues, ranging across the whole field of literary and cultural studies: two books on the mass media, *Communications* (1962) and *Television: Technology and Cultural Form* (1974b); three on drama, the entirely new *Modern Tragedy* (1966), and extensively reworked and revised versions of two earlier books, *Drama from Ibsen to Brecht* (1973a) and the second edition of *Drama in Performance* (1968); three studies in what might conventionally be considered literary criticism, *The English Novel: From Dickens to Lawrence* (1974), *George Orwell* (1971a) and *The Country and the City* (1973b); and a study in socio-historical philology, *Keywords* (1976a).

This last work represents an obvious continuation of the keywords motif in *Culture and Society* itself. The two studies of the mass media also further extend discussions originally broached in Williams's earlier work. Both seek to advance a critique of existing mass media institutions and texts that avoids the disabling cultural elitism characteristic not only of Leavisism but also of much available Marxist commentary; both seek thereby to identify the institutional forms which might sustain a properly democratic communications system. As Williams insisted in *Television*, the new televisual technologies 'are the contemporary tools of the long revolution towards an educated and participatory democracy' (Williams, 1974b:151). As we noted in the previous chapter, the studies of the English novel and of the modern drama each enabled a further refinement of the notion of 'structure of feeling'. In the work on drama, moreover, as in that on television, a new awareness of the social conventionality of form, and of the interrelationship between technology and form, is brought to bear. Dramatic convention, Williams writes, 'is . . . often, just this question of a relation between form and performance . . . to put the matter in this way is to realize also that it is a question of audiences; it is there, in the theatre as a social institution, that conventions are really made' (Williams, 1973a:398). The approach to television as a cultural form prompted Williams to a novel treatment of televisual programming as entailing not a sequence of discrete programmes but rather a total broadcasting 'flow' (Williams, 1974a:90). Williams's coupling of the problem of cultural form to that of cultural technology clearly drew attention, in the case of both television studies and drama studies, to the materiality of what were, in orthodoxly Marxist terms at least, 'ideal' superstructures. This led him, in turn, to a simultaneous rejection both of technological determinism and of the notion of a determined technology, and thence to a much more complex understanding of the notion of determination itself (ibid.:130). The chronological overlap between Williams's work in theatre studies and that on the mass media is thus by no means merely 'coincidental'. Disparate though the work might appear, it proceeds along clearly connected lines of inquiry. And these connections are empirical and substantive as well as theoretical and methodological. As Williams had already noted in the 'Conclusion' to *Drama from Ibsen to Brecht*: 'drama is no longer coexistent with theatre . . . The largest audience for drama, in our own world, is in the cinema and on television' (Williams, 1973a:399).

The Politics of Criticism

The cumulative effect of these apparently quite diverse lines of inquiry would finally be registered in *Marxism and Literature* itself. But that work is nonetheless not the 'extraordinary theoretical "coming out"', in which 'Williams finally admits the usefulness of Marxism' (Turner, 1990:65), that Turner takes it to be. Much more appropriate is O'Connor's emphasis on 'a *fundamental* theoretical continuity although there were shifts and changes' (O'Connor, 1989:103). One might well substitute 'developments' for 'shifts and changes' here. For, as we have noted, there *are* real developments—in the conceptualisation of structure of feeling, in the stress on the materiality of form, in that on the interconnectedness of form and technology—between *The Long Revolution* and *Marxism and Literature*. These arise, furthermore, within what is very obviously a rapidly changing intellectual and political context, that of what might loosely be termed 'the Sixties'. And it is this changing context, as much as any immanent theoretical development, which most clearly marks the diffference between *The Long Revolution* and *Marxism and Literature*.

Writing on the British New Left, Peter Sedgwick distinguished between what he termed the 'Old New Left', which formed from out of the political crises of 1956, and the 'New New Left', for whom the central political experience was that of 1968 (Sedgwick, 1976). Williams had belonged to the first formation, of course, and had played a central role in its evolution. In a number of important respects, his work both echoed and helped to form the sensibility of that early New Left: for example, his interest in culture as creative rather than merely epiphenomenal; in the particularities of the British experience, as distinct from the abstract 'internationalism' of the Russophile Communists; in the complex realities of contemporary working–class life understood by neither Leavisite nor Communist dogma; and in the potential for a socialism that would be, at once, both popular and democratic. The New New Left, by contrast, found its inspiration in the May '68 events in Paris, in the Vietnam Solidarity Campaign, the Prague Spring and the revolt on the campuses. Where the Old New Left had attempted to preserve the particularities of the British national experience from Stalinist internationalism, this New New Left spurned nationalism in general, and the peculiarities of the English especially, in favour of an uncompromising internationalism which took as its primary political responsibility solidarity with the Vietnamese Revolution. Where the Old New Left had situated itself somewhere in the political space between the left wing of the Labour Party and the liberalising wing of the Communist Party, this New New Left rejected both Labourism and Communism in favour of various 'ultraleftisms', Guevarism, Maoism, Trotskyism. Where the Old New Left had sought to counterpose 'experience' and 'culture' to Communist dogmatism, this New New Left discovered in the various continental European 'Western Marxisms' a type of 'Theory' which could be counterposed both to the empiricism of English bourgeois culture and to the pragmatism of the British Labour Party.

At this point, it might be as well to elaborate a little both on the history of Western Marxism itself and on that of its British and Anglophone receptions. The term 'Western Marxism' was coined by the French philosopher Maurice Merleau-Ponty to describe the tradition of 'critical' Marxism that developed in western Europe, and especially in Germany, Italy and France, by way of a more or less deliberate reaction against official Communist, 'scientific' Marxism (Merleau-Ponty, 1974:ch.2). This was an intellectual tradition the characteristic thematics of which were human agency, subjective consciousness, philosophical 'totality', and hence also 'culture'. As Perry Anderson observes: 'Western marxism as a whole . . . came to concentrate overwhelmingly on study of *superstructures* . . . It was culture that held the central focus of its attention' (Anderson, 1976:75–6). At its point of origin in the early 1920s, in the work of Georg Lukács, Karl Korsch and Antonio Gramsci, this stress on agency and consciousness had served to underwrite a leftist rejection of the political fatalism implicit in more orthodoxly Marxist economic determinisms. But as that moment of revolutionary optimism failed, then so the emphasis had shifted towards an analysis of the system-supportive nature of cultural legitimations. Such motifs are present from the very beginning, for example in Lukács's theory of reification (Lukács, 1971:83–110) and, by some readings, in Gramsci's theory of hegemony (Gramsci, 1971:210–76). But they become much more apparent in later formulations, perhaps most strikingly so in the critique of the Enlightenment and of the capitalist 'culture industry' developed by the major theorists of the Frankfurt School, Theodor Adorno and Max Horkheimer (Adorno and Horkheimer, 1979:120–67). This shift from an initial celebration of the emancipatory potential of culture as human self-activity to a subsequent recognition of the debilitating and disabling power of culture as 'ideology' marks the historical trajectory of Western Marxist thought from the early 1920s to the 1960s. But it continues also as a recurrent tension within Western Marxism. In the work of Lukács's disciple Lucien Goldmann, for example, that tension runs between, on the one hand, a sociology of the world vision, which stresses the intellectual creativity of social classes and groups, and on the other, a sociology of the novel, which stresses the rigorous homology between the historical development of the novel form and that of the commodity market (Goldmann, 1964:89–102; 1975:7). In the existential Marxism of Jean-Paul Sartre there is an analogous tension between a determination to vindicate the rationality of praxis, by demonstrating that human history can be understood entirely in terms of human projects, and a substantive emphasis on the ways in which real popular revolutions, confronted by scarcity, collapse into 'seriality' (Sartre, 1976:43–7; 1976–77:162).

Much of this work was unavailable in English translation until well into 'the Sixties'. Some of Lukács's later 'socialist realist' writings had in fact been translated in the early sixties (Lukács, 1962; 1963), Sartre's *Qu'est-ce que la littérature?* very promptly in 1950 (Sartre, 1950), and Goldmann's *Le Dieu caché* reasonably so in 1964 (Goldmann, 1964). But it was not until 1971 that substantial translations of the two 'key texts' in the Western Marxist tradition, Lukács's *Geschichte und Klassenbewusstsein* and Gramsci's *Quaderni del carcere*, were finally published (Lukács, 1971; Gramsci, 1971). Goldmann's book on Kant and Lukács's *Die Theorie des Romans* followed in the same year (Goldmann, 1971; Lukács, 1971a), Adorno and Horkheimer's *Die Dialektik der Aufklärung* a year later (Adorno and Horkheimer, 1972), the first volume of Sartre's *Critique de la raison dialectique* not until 1976. For the New New Left of the 1960s the lure of 'Theory' reached its apogee, however, not in any of these earlier 'humanist' Western Marxisms, but in the 'structural Marxism' of the French philosopher Louis Althusser. Althusser's *Pour Marx*, first published in French in 1966, had been very rapidly translated into English in 1969; an abridged edition of the co-authored *Lire le Capital*, first published in 1965, appeared in English in 1970 (Althusser and Balibar, 1970); *Lenin and Philosophy*, a collection of essays published separately in France during 1968 and 1969, followed a year later (Althusser, 1971). The *New Left Review* and its associated publishing house, New Left Books, came to provide an important conduit for these various Western Marxisms into British intellectual life. As the *Review*'s editor would later explain: 'NLR set out from the mid-sixties onwards to introduce the major intellectual systems of continental socialism in the post-classical epoch into the culture of the British Left' (Anderson, 1980: 149). In itself this contributed an important service not only to the British Left, but to British, and indeed Anglophone, intellectual life in general. If the tone was often far too reverential—Edward Thompson would later refer to the *Review*'s 'theoretical heavy breathing' (Thompson, 1978:405)—then the intent, to criticise, 'calmly and systematically, every one of the theoretical schools within "Western Marxism"' (Anderson, 1980:149) was entirely honourable. That said, we need also note that, for much of the late sixties and early seventies, the *Review*'s theoretical interests and sympathies were defined primarily in relation, not so much to Western Marxism per se, but rather to Althusserian 'theoretical practice'.

In Althusser's work, the characteristically Western Marxist tension between culture as praxis and culture as domination finally attains the unhappiest of all possible resolutions: neither abolished nor transcended, it is in effect repressed. Althusser's distinctive contribution to Western Marxism was to read Marxism as if it were a structuralism—much as his friend and colleague Jacques Lacan had read Freudian psychoanalysis—so that the older Western Marxist prioritisation of agency and praxis is altogether subsumed into a general theory of structural determination. In Althusser, culture is neither a superstructural effect nor the expression of the truth of a social totality, but rather an autonomous structure of 'ideology', with its own specific effectivity, located within and in relation to a wider structure of structures. In a much–quoted essay on 'Ideology and Ideological State Apparatuses', Althusser argued that ideology is necessarily embedded in institutions, or 'state apparatuses' as he termed them, and that its social function is that of the reproduction of the relations of production. Culture comes to be understood, then, in essentially structuralist terms, as '"constituting" concrete individuals as subjects' (Althusser, 1971:171). Ideology thereby represents, for Althusser, 'the imaginary relationship of individuals to their real conditions of existence' (ibid.:162). It was this peculiar hybrid of Marxism and structuralism that would excite the most extreme of New New Left enthusiasms, and yet simultaneously propel many of the Old New Left towards the most vehement of animosities toward 'continental Theory'. Moreover, Althusserianism appeared to have some peculiar purchase on the field of literary and cultural studies. Since art, though not itself an ideology according to Althusser, is nonetheless an allusion to ideology (Althusser, 1971:122), it becomes possible to read literature 'ideologically'. Althusser himself had developed a theory of symptomatic reading, which sought to reconstruct the 'problematic' of the text (Althusser and Balibar, 1970:30–4), that is, the structure of determinate absences and presences which occasion it. For the major Althusserian literary critics, Pierre Macherey in France (1978) and Terry Eagleton in England (1976), the new literary science would be directed at analogous readings of literary texts, thereby revealing ideology itself as the real object of literary studies. It was a project which would inspire nothing but scorn in Thompson: 'to suppose this to advance a "science" of materialist aesthetics is to calumniate both science and materialism' (Thompson, 1978:358).

The shift between the two New Left formations had been prefigured by the distinctly acrimonious transfer of the editorship of the *New Left Review* from Stuart Hall to Perry Anderson during 1962. Williams's own role at this time is interesting: he chose to act as a mediator between the two groups and thus, in effect, helped to secure the succession for the group around Anderson (Williams, 1979a:365). It was not that Williams positively endorsed the changes in style and content proposed by Anderson and his collaborators. It was rather 'a survival strategy that I mainly argued' (ibid.:366). For many on the Old New Left, however, this new political generation remained incorrigibly alien. For Thompson, settling old and not so old scores in the wonderfully vindictive 'Foreword' to *The Poverty of Theory*, the ten years after 1968 had been 'a time for reason to sulk in its tent', a time when 'Every pharisee was being more revolutionary than the next; some of them have made such hideous faces that they are likely to be stuck like that for life' (Thompson, 1978:ii). It had also been a time in which he had quietly joined the Labour Party. There is, no doubt, much to be admired in Thompson's polemic against Anderson's *New Left Review*, and by extension against the entire generation of '68. Doubtless, the *Review*'s encounter with Western Marxism had produced an at times hair-raising theoreticism; doubtless, Third World guerrilla movements had provided a bizarrely improbable model for radical politics in an advanced capitalist society; doubtless, much of what Thompson had to say about Althusserian 'structural Marxism' contained more than a grain of truth. But the depth of Thompson's disdain for 'those barrels of enclosed Marxisms which stand, row upon row, in the corridors of Polytechnics and Universities' (ibid.:383) suggests a distinct lack of both political charity and intellectual generosity.

While Thompson, and others, continued to beat 'the bounds of "1956"' (ibid.:384), Williams's own political evolution followed a rather different route. As early as 1965 he had joined the Vietnam Solidarity Campaign, by far the more 'militant' of the main bodies organising in opposition to American involvement in Vietnam. That Williams's political sympathies, from 1968 on, lay with the second generation of New Left intellectuals became increasingly apparent. He shared much of the *New Left Review*'s interest in Western Marxism, as essays on Goldmann, Gramsci and Sebastiano Timpanero, published in the *Review* in 1971, 1973 and 1978 respectively, clearly attest (Williams, 1971b; 1973c; 1978a). Indeed, in the Introduction to *Marxism and Literature* he would recall that 'I felt the excitement of contact with . . . new Marxist work . . . As all this came in, during the sixties and early seventies . . . an argument that had drifted into deadlock . . . in the late thirties and forties, was being vigorously and significantly reopened' (Williams, 1977a:4). Williams shared, too, the New New Left's deep and growing hostility to the Labour Party. Writing in the 'Retrospect and Prospect' to the third edition of *Communications*, he would conclude with some bitterness, of the experience of Labour governments, that 'most of the serious proposals were contemptuously pushed aside . . . The most plausible formation for intermediate reform has thus . . . not only defaulted on its own best purposes but . . . has shown itself . . . to be an active part of the very system which it has appeared to oppose' (Williams, 1976b:181–2). The contrast between Williams's *Marxism and Literature* and Thompson's *The Poverty of Theory*, which were published within a year of each other, is in fact especially telling: in their relations with this younger generation of radical intellectuals, it was, paradoxically, E. P. Thompson, the self-proclaimed scourge of sectaries, whose habits both of style and of thought remained by far the more sectarian.

But for all Williams's 'leftism', his is a movement in relation to an already established position, an evolution rather than a sudden 'coming out', and one that had been well under way long before 1977. It is most actively prefigured in *Modern Tragedy,* first published as early as 1966, and in *The Country and the City,* written during 1971 and first published in 1973. Both books were written in deliberate reaction against the predominant conservatism of Cambridge English studies (Williams, 1979a:243–4, 304). In *Modern Tragedy* Williams would argue, against the weight of contemporary academic opinion, for the significance of those everyday 'modern experiences that most of us call tragic' (Williams, 1979b:14). In *The Country and the City,* he would argue, once again against the weight of contemporary academic interpretation, for the relevance of 'questions of historical fact' (Williams, 1973b:12) to a critique of various mythologised accounts of rural life, initially those represented in the tradition of English country-house poetry. In both books the relevant experience is understood as essentially social and historical. Hence, for example, the judgement on Jonson and Carew that 'It is what the poems are: not country life but social compliment; the familiar hyperboles of the aristocracy and its attendants' (ibid.:33). Hence, too, the insistence on 'the connections between revolution and tragedy' (Williams, 1979b:64), on the ways in which the 'social fact' of revolution can become the 'structure of feeling' of tragedy (ibid.:65). In both books there is an often quite explicit identification with the fate of Third World peasant revolutionary movements. In *Modern Tragedy* these are invoked in such a fashion as to call into question the ultimate validity even of the long revolution itself: 'Our interpretation of revolution as a slow and peaceful growth . . . is at best a local experience . . . at worst a sustained false consciousness' (ibid.:79). In *The Country and the City* their successes provide the book with its concluding vindication: 'the "rural idiots" and the "barbarians and semi-barbarians" have been, for the last forty years, the main revolutionary force in the world' (Williams, 1973b:304). This is, in truth, a kind of Leavisite Maoism, at once culturalist in its critical methodology, revolutionist in its politics.

Culture and Hegemony

In Williams's earlier, 'left culturalist' writings, the 'deep community' that is culture simultaneously transcends class and is yet irredeemably marked by it. For all the eloquence with which this position is argued, it remains quite fundamentally incoherent: the competing claims of commonality and difference, culture and class, Leavisism and Marxism, form a circle which stubbornly refuses to be squared. But in the later, 'cultural materialist', phase of his work it finally became possible for Williams to explain, to his own satisfaction at least, how it could be that structures of feeling are common to different classes, and yet nonetheless represent the interests of some particular class. In this later phase, Williams's engagement with Western Marxism, and with various forms of Third Worldist 'ultraleftism', parallels, but nonetheless neither reduplicates nor inspires, that of Anderson's New New Left. Initially, this engagement meant little more than a recognition that not all Marxisms were necessarily economically determinist, and a corollary discovery of theoretical preoccupations similar to his own in the work of individual Western Marxist writers: the obviously important instance here is that of Lucien Goldmann. Later, however, it came to entail a much more positive redefinition of Williams's own theoretical stance: here, the encounter with Gramsci becomes absolutely central. As Williams would insist in *Marxism and Literature*: 'Gramsci's . . . work is one of the major turning-points in Marxist cultural theory' (Williams, 1977a:108). Let us consider each in turn, both in their own right and by way of their influence over Williams.

Goldmann's 'sociology of literature' had been widely translated into English. Goldmann himself had visited Britain on more than one occasion, and his work had come to command a considerable respect on the British intellectual left. Very much under the influence of the early Lukács, Goldmann had sought to substitute a 'social totality' model for the orthodoxly Marxist base/superstructure model. Hence, for Goldmann: 'It is when he replaces the work in a historical evolution which he studies as a whole, and when he relates it to the social life of the time at which it was written—which he also looks upon as a whole—that the enquirer can bring out the work's objective meaning' (Goldmann, 1964:8). In his earlier writings at least, Goldmann conceives of this relationship between literature and society, text and context, as essentially one of 'homology', and one typically 'mediated', moreover, through the 'world vision' of a social class or group. By the term 'world vision', Goldmann refers to 'the whole complex of ideas, aspirations and feelings which links together the members of a social group' (ibid.:17). Such world visions, he insists, can exist on two different planes: 'that of the *real* consciousness of the group . . . or that of their *coherent* exceptional expression in great works of philosophy or art' (Goldmann, 1969:130). Goldmann's coupling of coherence with exceptionality is fundamental to his argument: the coherent 'expression' in art of what is in quotidian life only ever incoherent thereby represents the '*maximum of potential consciousness*' (ibid.:103) of the group or class to which the artist belongs. This notion of the world vision is employed by Goldmann in his early study of Kant, and with considerable erudition in his major work on Pascal and Racine, *The Hidden God.* The efficacy with which Goldmann had been able to elucidate the internal structures of the Jansenist 'tragic vision', at work in both Pascal's *Pensées* and Racine's drama, suggested the value of this concept of the world vision not only to Williams, but to many others on the British intellectual left.

Williams's own interest in Goldmann is acknowledged most clearly in the obituary he wrote for the *New Left Review.* His fundamental response had been a recognition of affinity: he and Goldmann were 'exploring many of the same areas with many of the same concepts' (Williams, 1980:20). So Williams points to the similarities between his and Goldmann's conceptions of structure (ibid.:22–3), between the notion of structure of feeling and that of the world vision. In so far as there is difference between them, however, Williams concedes only a little to Goldmann: certainly, there are concepts, such as that of the 'collective subject', which we ought 'to test in practice' (ibid.:28); but the approach is nonetheless 'in some ways static', 'too large in its categories' (ibid.:26) to come very close to actual literature. For Williams, Goldmann's concept of the 'world vision' is too often 'a summary of doctrines', and as such, 'often some distance from the real structures and processes of literature' (ibid.:24). In *Marxism and Literature* the response is much the same: Goldmann's work is 'very important' (Williams, 1977a:106), his analysis of the collective subject 'most interesting' (ibid.:195); but explanation in terms of homology suffers from 'an extreme selectivity' (ibid.:106), and abstracted notions of coherence or integration obscure the reality of 'radical tension and disturbance, even actual and irresolvable contradiction' (ibid.:197). What Williams discovers in Goldmann (and in Lukács) is something much more akin to likemindedness than to inspiration: his own theoretical position, independently arrived at, and very much in isolation from continental European Marxism, is not so much challenged as confirmed, both by their insights and by what he perceives to be their deficiencies. The response to Gramsci, however, is of an altogether different order.

A single, slim volume of Gramsci's political writings had been translated into English during the 1950s (Gramsci, 1957), a limited critical debate had followed during the 1960s (cf. Merrington, 1968), and an English translation of Fiori's biography of Gramsci had been published in 1970 (Fiori, 1970). But there had been nothing even remotely equivalent to the positive avalanche of Gramsci scholarship, and Gramsci polemic, witnessed over the last twenty years. The first English publication of selections from Gramsci's *Prison Notebooks* was a major intellectual event, then, and was certainly taken as such in Williams's work. As is now well known, Gramsci had substituted for the more orthodoxly Marxist base/superstructure model a civil society/political society model, where the latter term refers to the coercive elements within the wider social totality, the former to the non-coercive. Hence the famous formula 'State = political society + civil society, in other words hegemony protected by the armour of coercion' (Gramsci, 1971:263). The term hegemony here refers to the processes by which a system of values and beliefs supportive of the existing ruling class becomes permeated throughout the whole of society. Hegemony is thus a value–consensus, and one very often embodied in common sense, but constructed, nonetheless, in the interests of the ruling class. Every state, Gramsci argues, 'is ethical in as much as one of its most important functions is to raise the great mass of the population to a particular cultural and moral level . . . which corresponds . . . to the interests of the ruling class' (ibid.:258). The schools, the courts, but also 'a multitude of other so-called private initiatives and activities', together form what Gramsci terms 'the apparatus of the political and cultural hegemony of the ruling classes' (ibid.). The functioning of this apparatus is essentially the work of intellectuals, whom Gramsci characterises as 'the dominant group's "deputies" exercising the subaltern functions of social hegemony and political government' (ibid.:12). Gramsci distinguishes between 'organic' intellectuals on the one hand, that is, the type of intellectual which each major social class creates for itself so as to 'give it homogeneity and an awareness of its own function' (ibid.:5), and traditional intellectuals on the other, that is, 'categories of intellectuals already in existence . . . which seem to represent . . . historical continuity' (ibid.:7). Hegemony is never in principle either uncontested or absolute, but is only ever an unstable equilibrium, ultimately open to contestation by alternative social forces. For Gramsci, the central political problem therefore becomes that of the creation of a layer of organic working-class intellectuals capable of leading their own class in this battle for counter-hegemony.

Williams was impressed both by Gramsci's work on intellectuals, which seemed to him an 'encouraging' and 'experimental' model for work in the sociology of culture (Williams, 1977a:138), and by the wider implications of the theory of hegemony itself. The significance of the latter had registered initially in an essay written for the *New Left Review* in 1973, entitled 'Base and Superstructure in Marxist Cultural Theory' (Williams, 1980:37). But in *Marxism and Literature*, the argument is elaborated upon at much greater length. The first and last chapters respectively of the book's first part are devoted to two key concepts, and two keywords, deriving respectively from Leavisism and Marxism: 'Culture' and 'Ideology'. In a subsequent chapter, Williams argues for the theoretical superiority over each of these of the Gramscian notion of hegemony:

> 'Hegemony' goes beyond 'culture' . . . in its insistence on relating the 'whole social process' to specific distributions of power and influence . . . Gramsci therefore introduces the necessary recognition of dominance and subordination in what has still, however, to be recognized as a whole process. It is in just this recognition of the *wholeness* of the process that the concept of 'hegemony' goes beyond 'ideology'. What is decisive is not only the conscious system of ideas and beliefs, but the whole lived social process as practically organized by specific and dominant meanings and values. (Williams, 1977a:108–9)

For Williams, Gramsci's central achievement consists in the articulation of a culturalist sense of the wholeness of culture with a more typically Marxist sense of the interestedness of ideology. Thus hegemony is 'in the strongest sense a "culture", but a culture which has to be seen as the lived dominance and subordination of particular classes' (ibid.:110). Understood thus, culture is no longer either 'superstructural', as the term had normally been defined in the Marxist tradition, or 'ideological', in the more generally Marxist or more specifically Althusserian definition. On the contrary, 'cultural tradition and practice . . . are among the basic processes', which need to be seen 'as they are . . . without the characteristic straining to fit them . . . to other and determining . . . economic and political relationships' (ibid.:111). Whether all of this remains exactly faithful to Gramsci's own intent seems open to some doubt. Gramsci himself repeatedly deploys the distinction between 'structure' and 'super-structure', and, while recognising the 'complex, contradictory or discordant' qualities of the latter, nonetheless insists that the '*ensemble* of the superstructures is the reflection of the *ensemble* of the social relations of production' (Gramsci, 1971:366). But as Stuart Hall has somewhat cynically observed of the *Prison Notebooks*: 'What was undoubtedly a limitation from a textual point of view—namely, the fragmentary nature of his writings—was . . . a positive advantage' (Hall, 1991:8) for subsequent Gramscian theory. Whatever the original authorial intention (and this is by no means at all self-evident), Williams's appropriation of Gramsci finally delivers that resolution of culturalist and Marxist thematics hitherto denied him.

In one respect, at least, Williams's reading of Gramsci is indeed unusually faithful to its object: for both the Italian revolutionary and his Welsh interpreter, it is the counter-hegemonic moment that is especially significant. Hence Williams's attempt to distinguish be-tween those practices, experiences, meanings and values that are part of the effectively dominant culture and those that are not. The dominant or hegemonic culture, Williams reminds us, 'is always an active process', an organisation of often quite disparate meanings, 'which it specifically incorporates in a significant culture' (ibid.:115). Rehearsing an argument first broached in *Culture and Society*, he points once again to the decisive importance of 'selective tradition' in the effective operation of such processes of incorporation: 'tradition is in practice the most evident expression of the dominant and hegemonic pressures and limits. It is always more than an inert historicized segment; indeed it is the most powerful practical means of incorporation' (ibid.). In *Marxism and Literature*, however, tradition is seen not only as selective but also as necessarily dependent upon identifiable institutions, on the one hand, and what Williams terms 'formations', that is, intellectual or artistic movements and tendencies, on the other (ibid.:117–20). This double stress on institutions and formations is explored at greater length in *Culture*, where Williams advances a preliminary historical typology both of cultural institutions, ranging from the 'instituted artist' of relatively early societies to the 'post-market institutions' of contemporary public and private patronage (Williams, 1981:33–56), and of formations, ranging from early forms of internal organisation, such as the bardic rules of the Welsh court poets and the medieval craft guilds, to such twentieth–century 'paranational' formations as the avant-garde (ibid.:57–86). For all this attention to hegemonic traditions, institutions and formations, Williams remains insistent that, at the level of 'historical' as distinct from 'epochal' analysis, that is, at the level of movement rather than system, there is much in any lived culture that cannot be reduced to the dominant (Williams, 1977a:121). Here, Williams dissents sharply from the implied consensualism of both Althusserian theories of ideology and the then current sociological versions of 'the dominant ideology thesis': '*no mode and therefore no dominant social order*', he writes, '*and therefore no dominant culture ever in reality includes or exhausts all human practice, human energy, and human intention*' (ibid.:125).

Williams's initial theorisation of the alternatives to hegemony had been broached in the 1973 *New Left Review* essay, where he had sought to distinguish between 'alternative' and 'oppositional', 'residual' and 'emergent' cultural elements (Williams, 1980:39–42). The terminology recurs both in *Marxism and Literature* and in *Culture*. By 'residual' Williams means not so much the simply 'archaic', defined as 'that which is wholly recognized as an element of the past', but rather those cultural elements, external to the dominant culture, which nonetheless continue to be lived and practised as an active part of the present 'on the basis of the residue . . . of some previous social and cultural institution or formation' (Williams, 1977a:122). Unlike the archaic, the residual may be oppositional or, at least, alternative in character. Thus Williams distinguishes organised religion and the idea of rural community, which are each predominantly residual, from monarchy, which is merely archaic. But it is the properly 'emergent', that is, those genuinely new meanings and values, practices, relationships and kinds of relationship, which are substantially alternative or oppositional to the dominant culture (ibid.:123), that most interest Williams. For Williams, as for Gramsci, the primary source of an emergent culture is likely to be the formation of a new social class. But there is also a second source of emergence: 'alternative perceptions of others, in immediate relationships; new perceptions and practices of the material world' (ibid.:126). For Williams, as for Gramsci, the exemplary contemporary instance of a new social class is that of the development of the modern working class. At the second level, however, which Williams terms 'the excluded social [human] area' (ibid.), a level which often remains peculiarly pertinent to the analysis of artistic and intellectual movements, the situation is much less clear. As Williams writes in *Culture*: 'No analysis is more difficult than that which, faced by new forms, has to try to determine whether these are new forms of the dominant or are genuinely emergent' (Williams, 1981:205). This testimony to complexity is no mere rhetorical gesture on Williams' part. Quite the contrary: his work both in drama studies and in media studies, that is, in each of the two areas of substantive cultural analysis which had come most to concern him, had made Williams all too aware of the difficulties entailed in distinguishing the properly emergent from the merely novel.

Theoretically at least, Williams is able, in *Marxism and Literature*, to offer an unusually interesting formulation of the problem itself, if not necessarily of the ways in which it might be resolved. Here, he redeploys and significantly redefines his earlier notion of 'structure of feeling'. An emergent culture, Williams argues, unlike either the dominant or the residual, requires not only distinct kinds of immediate cultural practice, but also and crucially 'new forms or adaptations of forms'. Such innovation at the level of form, he continues, 'is in effect a *pre-emergence*, active and pressing but not yet fully articulated, rather than the evident emergence which could be more confidently named' (Williams, 1977a:126). And it is precisely at this level of the pre-emergent that the concept of structure of feeling is brought back into play. From *The Long Revolution* onwards, as we have seen, Williams had used the term to denote both the immediately experiential and the generationally specific aspects of artistic process. In *Marxism and Literature*, both emphases are retained, but are conjoined to a quite new stress on cultural pre-emergence. In this reformulation, the experiential remains at odds with official, 'formal' culture precisely in so far as it is indeed genuinely new: 'practical consciousness is what is actually being lived . . . not only what it is thought is being lived' (ibid.:130–1). And similarly, the generationally specific remains different from the experience of previous generations precisely in so far as it too is indeed genuinely new. Structures of feeling, writes Williams, in an unusually arresting formulation,

> can be defined as social experiences *in solution*, as distinct from other social semantic formations which have been *precipitated* and are more evidently and more immediately available . . . The effective formations of most actual art relate to already manifest social formations, dominant or residual, and it is primarily to emergent formations . . . that the structure of feeling, *as solution*, relates. (ibid.:133–4)

Structures of feeling are no longer, then, in any sense 'the culture' of a period: they are, rather, precisely those particular elements within the more general culture which most actively anticipate subsequent mutations in the general culture itself; in short, they are quite specifically counter-hegemonic.

At one level, this distinctly Gramscian reformulation of the notion of 'structure of feeling' merely recaptures something of what Williams had all along intended: the problem of the knowable community in the English novel, and the naturalistic revolution in the modern theatre, each delimit a distinct structure of feeling only in so far as they are indeed genuinely innovatory. But in each case, these respectively pre-emergent qualities are never fully theorised. It is as if the concept itself is still pre-emergent, and requires the encounter with Gramsci for precipitation. Moreover, the substantive question of the precise interplay between the emergent or pre-emergent, on the one hand, and novelty within the dominant, on the other, in both mass media forms and modernist avant-garde forms, was to become especially pressing for Williams only in his later works. The issue is broached very clearly in *Culture*. But it becomes absolutely central to the two major works of the 1980s, the 1983 reworking of the long revolution analysis, *Towards 2000* (1983), and the posthumously published and sadly unfinished *The Politics of Modernism* (1989a). Both books attempt to reformulate the earlier aspiration to community and to culture as a whole way of life, by way of a critique of 'postmodern' appropriations of modernism itself and of the popular mass media.

In *Towards 2000*, Williams shows how postmodernism effectively collapses the distinction between minority and mass arts: 'There are very few absolute contrasts left between a "minority culture" and "mass communications" . . . many minority institutions and forms have adapted . . . with enthusiasm, to modern corporate capitalist culture' (Williams, 1983:134, 140). The older modernisms, which had once threatened to destabilise the certainties of bourgeois life, have been transformed, he argues, into a new '"post-modernist" establishment', which 'takes human inadequacy . . . as self-evident' (ibid.:141). The deep structures of this now dominant postmodernism are present, moreover, in effectively popular cultural forms, such as film, television and fiction: 'these debased forms of an anguished sense of human debasement . . . have become a widely distributed "popular" culture that is meant to confirm both its own and the world's destructive inevitabilities' (ibid.:141–2). The 'pseudo-radicalism' of 'the negative structures of post-modernist art' (ibid.:145) is thus neither pre-emergent nor emergent, but rather a moment of novelty, indeed perhaps the institutionalisation of novelty itself, within the already dominant culture. As Williams would observe in *The Politics of Modernism*, the dominant institutions themselves 'now incorporate or impose' such 'easy labels of radicalism' (Williams, 1989a:176). But if the dominant culture has indeed so mutated, then Williams is able also to detect a more properly innovatory, pre-emergent 'structure of feeling'—though the term itself is not actually used—in the politics of the contemporary new social movements (Williams, 1983:250).

Determination, Forms and Practices

Williams's 'Base and Superstructure' essay had signalled not only a new reading of Gramsci but also an attempt to recast the base/superstructure formula itself. He had argued for a 'revaluation' of each of the three terms in the formula, 'base', 'superstructure' and 'determination', so that: the first would now denote the primary production of society itself and of people themselves, rather than the merely 'economic'; the second, the whole range of cultural practices, rather than a merely secondary and dependent 'content'; and the third, the 'setting of limits and exertion of pressures', rather than predetermined causation (Williams, 1980:34–5). The last proposition is very much the same as that advanced the following year in *Television: Technology and Cultural Form*. In *Marxism and Literature*, however, the argument is taken further, but in a direction that leads, perhaps paradoxically, very much away from, rather than toward, the more classically Marxist formulations of the problem. Once again determination is taken to mean the setting of limits and exertion of pressures (Williams, 1977a:87); once again production is understood as applying to a much wider realm than the merely economic, so that the 'productive forces' are 'all and any activities in the social process as a whole' (ibid.:93). But the notions of 'base' and 'superstructure', which had acquired an entirely temporary and very much conditional legitimacy in the 1973 essay, are here consigned to a theoretical oblivion very like that in *Culture and Society*: 'contrary to the development in Marxism, it is not "the base" and "the superstructure" that need to be studied, but specific and indissoluble real processes' (ibid.:82). Ironically, Williams is very much concerned to invoke Marx himself against subsequent Marxism on precisely this point. 'Marx's original criticism', he insists, 'had been mainly directed against the *separation* of "areas" of thought and activity . . . The common abstraction of "the base" and "the superstructure" is thus a radical persistence of the modes of thought which he attacked' (ibid.:78). It is difficult to avoid the suspicion that here, at least, Williams protests too much. And yet there is a strong sense in which his position is indeed 'Marxist'. For this is no simple return to the argument of *Culture and Society*, but rather the development of an entirely new argument, by which Williams seeks to convict Marxism, in the telling phrase of his 1979 *New Left Review* interlocutors, of 'not so much . . . an excess but . . . a deficit of materialism' (Williams, 1979a:350). What the base/superstructure formula fails to acknowledge, he charges, is precisely the materiality of the superstructures themselves. Hence the characteristically ruthless judgement that 'The concept of "superstructure" was . . . not a reduction but an evasion' (Williams, 1977a:93).

Superstructure, Williams concludes, and other, related usages within Marxist discourse, such as 'ideology' or 'the realm of art and ideas', each misrepresent what are in fact real and material activities as somehow unreal and immaterial. None of these activities can then be grasped as they are: 'as real practices, elements of a whole material social process; not a realm or a world or a superstructure, but many and variable productive practices, with specific conditions and intentions' (ibid.:94). The way forward, he insists, is 'to look at our actual productive activities without assuming in advance that only some of them are material' (ibid.). If Williams retains a concept of determination, then, as he certainly does, it is nonetheless a concept of multiple determination, much more akin to the culturalist sense of a whole way of life than to the Marxist notion of a determining base and a determined superstructure. But that whole way of life is now both thoroughly material and thoroughly marked by the impress of power and domination, in all its particular aspects. This stress on the materiality of cultural production had been a recurrent theme in Williams's work from *The Long Revolution* onwards, most especially so in his writing on drama and on the mass media. But in *Marxism and Literature* it attains a much more explicit formulation than any hitherto.

In *Culture*, and in a 1978 essay published by the Yugoslav journal *Prilozi: Drustvenost Komunikacije*, the process would be taken even further, as Williams would seek to analyse means of communication as in themselves means of production (Williams, 1980:50–63; Williams, 1981:87–118). In *Marxism and Literature*, however, the argument leads immediately toward what is in effect a 'deconstruction' of probably the most sacred of all Leavisite categories, that of 'Literature' itself. The specialising concept of 'Literature', Williams recognises, is an important instance of 'the aesthetic' (Williams, 1977a:150), and the aesthetic itself a specifically bourgeois evasion, by which art and thinking about art 'separate themselves . . . from the social processes within which they are . . . contained' (ibid.:154). To such evasions, and to their often transparently elitist ideological functions, Williams seeks to counterpose a stress on 'the multiplicity of writing' (ibid.:146), and on 'the variability, the relativity, and the multiplicity of actual cultural practice' (ibid.:153). In the third and final part of *Marxism and Literature*, and again in *Culture*, this would lead to an extended theorisation of the social processes of art and literature themselves.

This account is premised upon what is clearly the distinguishing proposition of cultural materialism, that of the materiality of cultural production. Drawing extensively on the work of the Russian Marxist semiotician V. N. Volosinov (1973), Williams argues for a theory of 'language as activity, as practical consciousness' (Williams, 1977a:36). Whether spoken or written, language is, for Williams, not a 'medium', in the sense of an intermediate communicative substance, mediating between thought and expression, but rather a constitutive element of material social practice (ibid.:158–9, 165). More particularly, 'Language is in fact a special kind of material practice: that of human sociality' (ibid.:165). Linguistic signification is then, for Williams as much as for any structuralist, a 'real and demonstrable activity' (ibid.:167), with its own distinctively material, and in a sense 'formal', properties. But signs are not thereby 'arbitary', as structuralism is wont to claim. Quite the contrary, they function within 'lived and living relationships', and it is these relationships, sociologically determinate rather than arbitrary in character, which in Williams's view *'make all formal meanings significant and substantial'* (ibid.:168). Moreover, Williams continues, the structuralist concept of the sign significantly occludes the distinction between speech and writing: 'Spoken words are a process of human activity using only immediate, constitutive, physical resources. Written words . . . are a form of material production, adapting non-human resources to a human end' (ibid.:169).

Writing, Williams argues, is better understood as 'notation' than as 'sign', since, unlike speech, it is at once both materially objectified and reproducible, and this reproducibility is itself necessarily dependent on the socio-cultural system within which the notation is operative (ibid.:146, 170). Such dependence is in fact much more characteristic of writing than of many other cultural techniques, such as dance, song and speech. As Williams observes in *Culture*: 'Writing . . . is wholly dependent on forms of specialized training, not only . . . for producers but also, and crucially, for receivers' (Williams, 1981:93). The French post-structuralist philosopher Jacques Derrida has charged the western philosophical tradition with adherence to a falsely 'logocentric' notion of language as 'voice', and of writing as the expression of speech, insisting to the contrary that the true nature of language is more clearly revealed in writing than in speech (Derrida, 1973:92; 1982:316). Derrida's critique of logocentrism runs interestingly parallel to Williams's own critique of 'expressivism' (Williams, 1977:165). But where Derrida, the prophet of *différance*, chooses to privilege writing over speech, it is Williams, ironically enough, who proves able to register this distinction, between speech and writing, word and notation, as quite simply difference. For Williams, moreover, though writing is not speech, and notation not expression, expression is nonetheless not thereby excluded from a 'fully social' theory of literature: 'the notations are relationships, expressed, offered, tested, and amended in a whole social process, in which device, expression, and the substance of expression are in the end inseparable' (Williams, 1977a:172).

Central to Williams's understanding of what any such fully social theory of literature might be is the concept of form. Williams's sense of the social conventionality of form, and of the interdependence of form, technique and technology, had emerged as much from his work in drama studies and television studies as from anywhere. In *Marxism and Literature*, Williams argues for the theoretical superiority of notions of form over mere 'genre-classification' (ibid.:185–6). For Williams, the problem of form is first, that of the historically variable relations between social modes and individual projects, and second, that of the specifiable material practices within which those relations are enacted (ibid.:187). Form, then, is not so much a matter of classification as of social relationship: 'it is . . . a social process which . . . becomes a social product. Forms are . . . the common property . . . of writers and audiences or readers, before any communicative composition can occur' (ibid.:187–8). Here, Williams's argument is primarily theoretical in character. In *Culture*, however, such theorisation is supplemented by a fairly lengthy and nuanced socio-formal analysis of the history of the drama (Williams, 1981:148–80) and by an attempt to distinguish three different 'levels of form', denoted respectively as 'modes', 'genres' and 'types'. Williams reserves the term 'mode' for those very general conventions, at the deepest level of form, for example the dramatic, the lyrical and the narrative, which, though socially and historically created, nonetheless persist through very different social orders (ibid.:194). He rehabilitates the term 'genre' to refer to that level of form which, though certainly enduring, has some definite dependence on epochal change between social orders, for example the genres of tragedy or comedy within the dramatic mode, or of epic and romance within the narrative (ibid.:195). Finally, he defines as 'types' those effective general forms which, in their characteristic distributions of interest, are typical only of a particular social order, as, for example, in the case of bourgeois drama or the realist novel (ibid.:196). At each of these levels, form is, of course, by definition reproducible; and for Williams, as for Althusser, culture is thereby necessarily reproductive (ibid.:184). But for Williams, as not for Althusser, culture is also necessarily productive: 'social orders and cultural orders must be seen as being actively made . . . unless there is . . . production and innovation, most orders are at risk' (ibid.:201). And at their furthest reach, as we have seen, such innovations in form will signify what is for Williams perhaps the most important of all cultural possibilities, that of an emergent structure of feeling.

What for Leavis had been a 'Literature', a canon of exemplary creative works, expressive of a national tradition, and what for Marxism had been an ideological superstructure of the economic system, becomes in Williams's cultural materialism a distinctive subset of socially specific, materially determinate, forms and practices. It is only a subset because the category 'Literature' denotes for Williams only a particular, socially valorised selection from the whole body of socially available writing, and writing in turn only one among many forms of cultural practice. Bereft of canon and national tradition alike, the obvious question arises as to what will become of authorship, in Leavisism the ultimate guarantee, in principle at least, of the authoritative meaning of the literary work. In its own assault on literary humanism, French structuralism had prosecuted a vigorous campaign against the notion of authorship. Arguing that literary texts should be understood in terms of intertextuality rather than supposed authorial intentions, Roland Barthes, for example, had polemically announced 'the death of the Author' (Barthes, 1977:148). Less polemically, but equally determinedly, Michel Foucault had elaborated upon this notion so as to explain authorship as a function of its various institutional uses (Foucault, 1977a:113–38). Such 'decentring' of the author is very obviously anticipated in Williams's own chapter 'The Social History of English Writers' in *The Long Revolution* (1965:254–70). And in *Marxism and Literature* Williams readily concedes the problematic status of the figure of the author (1977a:192). But for Williams authorship cannot be reduced to an effect either of textuality or of the institutionalised processing of texts. Rather, the central question remains, much as argued by Goldmann, that of the dynamic interrelationship between social formation, individual development and cultural creation: 'Taken together', he concludes, 'these . . . allow a fully constitutive definition of authorship' (ibid.:197). For Williams, then, the author as writer, though not as authoritative source or origin, remains, if not central, then at least not yet radically decentred. It is too easy to dismiss this as residual humanism: what matters here is Williams's refusal to reduce the moment of literary production to that of consumption. Where Barthes inaugurates the French section of what would later become, in Terry Eagleton's rather nice joke, the 'Readers' Liberation Movement' (Eagleton, 1986:181), Williams continues to hold firmly to the irreducibility of authorship and readership, either to each other or to an amorphous 'textuality', and to the necessarily material sociality of each, both in themselves and in relation to each other. 'In this at once social and historical perspective,' he writes, 'the abstract figure of "the author" is . . . returned to these varying *and in principle variable* situations, relationships, and responses' (Williams, 1977a:198).

In the 'Base and Superstructure' essay, Williams had worried that the Lukácsian concept of totality might too easily be emptied of any Marxist content, that is, of any notion of determination (Williams, 1980:36), thereby becoming almost trivially circular in effect. The obvious question arises as to whether or not his own cultural materialism might provide occasion for similar concern. Such concerns very obviously inspire Eagleton's view, to which we referred in chapter one, that Williams's position is essentially pre-Marxist. Writing in defence of the base/superstructure model, Eagleton insists that the classically Marxist version of that model is not, as Williams supposes, an ontological proposition about the materiality or immateriality of superstructures but rather a historical proposition as to the way in which some material activities, those denoted as 'the base', are more fundamentally determining within the social process than those other, equally material but nonetheless less causally effective, activities, denoted as 'the superstructure' (Eagleton, 1989a:168–9). In so far as Williams's cultural materialism rejects the base/superstructure model, then, Eagleton argues, it 'does indeed hold to a "circular" theory of the social formation, one in this respect little changed from his earlier work . . . Essentially Marxist concepts . . . were transplanted into the cultural realm to "materialize" cultural processes . . . so *intensifying* Williams's pre-Marxian "circularity"' (ibid.:171–2). There is a certain disingenuousness, nonetheless, to Eagleton's defence of 'classical Marxism': as he himself concedes, the 'vulgar Marxism' of Marx's own *German Ideology* did dematerialise the superstructure (ibid.:168); as, too, did the kind of Communist Marxism against which Williams had been obliged to define his own argument. In so far as cultural materialism does perhaps reinvent the wheel, as Eagleton charges (ibid.), then this suggests only the much greater propensity to collective amnesia among cultural theorists than among wheel-wrights. But Eagleton is right, nonetheless, to point to the circularity, indeed the deliberate circularity, of Williams's later position. In the 1973 essay itself Williams had attempted to circumvent any such fate through the invocation of class intentionality, so that social structure comes to be understood as ordered by 'the rule of a particular class' (Williams, 1980:36). By *Marxism and Literature*, however, even this latter, residual notion of the 'base' had finally been abandoned.

When the editors of the *New Left Review* raised with Williams exactly this question of circularity, he was quick to concede 'warm agreement' to the historical priority of some determinations over others; but quick also to reformulate the matter at issue in terms of 'the specificity of capitalism' (Williams, 1979a:140). In *Marxism and Literature* he had pointed to Marx's own distinction between 'production in general', that is, the human historical process by which we produce ourselves and our societies; and 'capitalist production', that is, commodity production on the basis of wage labour and capital (Williams, 1977a:90–1). It is the social reality of capitalism itself, Williams insists, which progressively reduces production in general to commodity production in particular; the base/superstructure formula in Marxism merely reproduces and replicates that reduction at the level of theory (ibid.:92). He repeats this argument in the *New Left Review* interview:

In the 20th century the exponents of capitalism have been the most insistent theorists of the causal primacy of economic production. If you want to be told that our whole existence is governed by the economy, go to the city pages of the bourgeois press—that is really how they see life. (Williams, 1979a:141)

Elsewhere, Williams adds a distinctly 'postmodern' inflection to this sense of the specificities of capitalism. For if capitalism begins by extruding cultural production, as also other forms of non-commodity production, from the economic 'base', it eventually proceeds, in the late twentieth century, to an effective reincorporation of much of our culture back into that 'base', but on terms very much dictated by the economy. This is the commodity culture of postmodernism, of course. And it is a culture which, in Williams's view, remains radically unamenable to analysis in terms of any base/superstructure metaphor. For Williams, cultural materialism is itself at one level a specific theoretical response to the cultural specificities of postmodern, advanced capitalism: 'cultural theory was not reworked as a critique within a theoretical tradition', he writes, 'but as a response to radical changes in the social relations of cultural process' (Williams, 1980:245). At a time when broadcasting and publishing, advertising and the press had already been transformed into major industries, it had simply become impossible, he continues, 'to see cultural questions as practically separable from political and economic questions, or to posit either second-order or dependent relations between them' (ibid.).

In the *Politics and Letters* interviews, Williams credits Lukács as the original proponent of this view that the priority of the economic is not so much a general feature of human social life as a distinguishing peculiarity of capitalism. But there are more obvious sources much closer to hand, surely, in that very same culturalist tradition which had first inspired *Culture and Society*. When Williams points—rightly in my view—to the complicity between Marxist theoretical reductionism on the one hand, and the real reductions of bourgeois reality on the other, he echoes something of Leavis's own judgement that Communism aims 'at completing the work of capitalism and its products' (Leavis, 1933:172). And behind Leavis there stands that whole tradition of Romantic and post-Romantic anti-utilitarianism to which we referred in chapter one. This tradition and its legacy in Williams's own early formulations—of 'structure of feeling', of the 'selective tradition', also in truth of the inadequacies of the base/superstructure thesis—remains much more actively present in the later cultural materialism than is often supposed. Indeed, Turner's judgement on *Marxism and Literature*, that Williams 'accepted his place within a Marxist tradition only to disappear into it' (Turner, 1990:68), is in fact perilously close to the exact opposite of the truth. What disappears in Williams's 'Marxism' is precisely the central but false tenet of virtually all hitherto existing Marxist cultural theory, that of a determining base and a determined superstructure; what appears in its place is a radically novel theoretical position, selectively appropriating both Marxist and culturalist traditions, so as to theorise not only its own distinctive subject matter, that is, the socio-semiotic systems of late capitalist society, but also the very conditions of its own theoretical novelty. The squared circle of Williams's own 'circularity' is thus a profoundly historicist response to his own historicity. In so far as Williams became a Marxist, then, it was only ever as a 'heretic in truth'—to borrow Eagleton's borrowing from Milton—whose return to the fold can only ever ensure that 'the fold will never be the same again' (Eagleton, 1989a:175). This is not so much a Marxism, then, as a post- Marxism; not so much a culturalism as a post-culturalism.

Williams's entire intellectual effort was organised around a continuing political project, that of a radically democratic, popular socialism, in which the idea of a common culture, truly made in common, might finally be realised. It was organised also around an enduring 'structure of feeling', which has three main categories: the centrality of culture, as both textual artefact and lived experience; the fundamental importance of serious intellectual work; and the persistent significance of class and community. Thus 'culture' came to mediate between intellectual work on the one hand, and class and community on the other, in Williams's own structure of feeling as surely as it had in his personal biography. Within the broad contours of this continuing political project and this continuing structure of feeling, Williams's work was to prove remarkably innovative. In his more general formulations of the theory of cultural materialism and in his later substantive work on postmodernity, Williams moved beyond both the left culturalisms of the Old New Left and the theoreticist Marxisms of the New New Left into what was surely a properly post-Marxist, post-culturalist theoretical terrain. The achievement is remarkable, but somehow unsurprising, for, of course, Williams *valued* change. This capacity for change, once described by Eagleton as an 'almost intuitive "prevention" of . . . new births' (Eagleton, 1976:35), was not simply a particular, contingent, personal strength. It was something which arose directly from his understanding of cultural analysis as the 'study of patterns and relationships, in a whole process' (Williams, 1965:119), with the stress placed equally on each of the latter two terms. An imagination such as his could not settle for beating the bounds, whether between disciplines or between generations, as unfortunately had Thompson's. Which is why, to engage in a comparison that is unavoidably invidious, Williams really was by far the most intellectually and politically significant figure to write about literature and culture in the English language during the twentieth century. As he himself observed: 'Marxism in Britain . . . in this field has not been an offshore island but a major contributor' (Williams, 1980:246). That this is so was in large part Williams's own personal accomplishment.

4

Applications and Implications

Williams's cultural materialism emerged from a sustained encounter between Leavisite literary criticism on the one hand, socialist politics on the other. It was never, however, merely an attempt either to politicise literature or to 'enculture' politics. In so far as such tendencies are present in Williams's work, and indeed they are, they bespeak not so much its particularity as its more generally representative quality. For the elision of politics and letters was, in fact, quite fundamentally constitutive not only of postwar British left intellectualism but also in some respects of the entire postwar British social-democratic settlement. As Alan Sinfield has interestingly observed:

> The hopes that have been placed in literature have been surprisingly close to the centre of the postwar settlement. The idea was that the benefits that the upper-class had customarily arranged for itself would now be generally available . . . So what had hitherto been . . . the culture of the leisure class was proclaimed as a universal culture. (Sinfield, 1989:2)

It would be surprising if Williams's work were not implicated in this more general culture of which it formed a part: as he himself once observed, his was 'an ordinary life, spanning the middle years of the twentieth century' (Williams, 1979b:13). But the originality of both the life and the work consist not in this elision between literature and politics, but in something close to its obverse: in the way in which

Williams ultimately chooses to 'deconstruct', to borrow a currently fashionable term, both left politics and literary criticism, both Marxism and Literature. This is a 'deconstruction', however, which clearly predates Derridean deconstruction proper. Williams's work had in practice long sought to problematise the socio-discursive boundaries both of political radicalism and of cultural work: hence his support for a 'new left', rather than the old left of the Communist and Labour parties; hence, too, his enthusiasm for the new proto-disciplines of cultural studies and media studies, rather than simply for 'Marxist literary criticism'. In each of these areas, Williams's own contribution was to prove formative, sometimes quite decisively so. In this chapter, then, we move to an account of the influence of cultural materialism, by turn, on cultural studies and on literary studies; in the next, to a brief discussion of its relevance to contemporary radical politics.

Cultural Materialism, Structuralism, Post-Structuralism

We have referred to Williams's work as in some sense a 'deconstruction', a reference which serves to remind us of the wider intellectual context within which cultural materialism had evolved. For, if Williams's work represents the central instance of an indigenously British critique of more traditional literary humanisms, then structuralism and post-structuralism perform analogous functions within French intellectual life. We have had occasion to refer to this French tradition, partly because of the obvious parallelism between British and French developments, but also partly because French theory came to exercise a considerable fascination for British intellectual radicalism from the mid–1960s onwards, that is, in precisely the period in which Williams was working towards a mature cultural materialism. Before proceeding, it might be as well to entertain a brief digression on the subject of French structuralism and its Anglophone reception. There are many different versions of structuralism, both in general and as applied to literature and culture in particular. But for our purposes, structuralism might best be defined as an approach to the study of human culture centred on the search for constraining patterns, or structures, which claims that individual phenomena have meaning only by virtue of their relation to other phenomena within

4 *Applications and Implications*

a systematic structure. More specifically, this general proposition has often been supplemented by the much more precise claim that the methods of structural linguistics can be successfully generalised so as to apply to all aspects of human culture (Robey, 1973:1–2). In France itself, Durkheim's work on 'primitive' religion (1976), and Saussure's on language (1974), first published in 1915 and 1916 respectively, directly anticipated the subsequent histories of the two academic disciplines most directly implicated in structuralism: anthropology on the one hand, and semiology, or the science of the study of signs, on the other. During the late 1950s and the early 1960s, a continuing tradition of post-Durkheimian anthropology came to coincide with a revival of Saussurean semiology, initiated in the first place by Roland Barthes, and with the translation of a series of texts from the Russian Formalist school of literary criticism, so as to generate what became the theoretical moment of French high structuralism. This was above all the moment of Barthes himself, the single most important, representative figure in French structuralism, an immensely prolific writer whose work as a literary critic, cultural sociologist and semiologist inspired considerable respect. But it was also that of the structural anthropology of Claude Lévi-Strauss, of Michel Foucault's archaeology of knowledge, and of Louis Althusser's structural Marxism.

Each of these structuralisms displayed a recurrent aspiration to scientificity. At the end of *The Archaeology of Knowledge*, however, Foucault confesses, uncomfortably, that his discourse 'is avoiding the ground on which it could find support' (Foucault, 1972b:205). The embarrassment is distinctive, but the problem is not. For Barthes, for Lévi-Strauss, for Althusser, as for Foucault, the central repressed problem had been throughout that of how to guarantee the scientificity of a knowledge that was, according to the logic of its own argument, either socially or intra-discursively located. No solution to this problem appeared possible from within structuralism. Hence the move by both Barthes and Foucault, during the 1970s, toward different versions of 'post-structuralism'. Hence, too, the meteoric rise to intellectual pre-eminence, during the same period, of Jacques Derrida. Each of these various post-structuralisms insisted that meaning could never finally be pinned down, not even by structuralism itself. Three main versions of post-structuralism thus emerged:

first, that type of literary 'deconstruction' practised by the later Barthes, and more influentially by Derrida; second, Foucault's middle–period writings on the theme of knowledge–power relations, which he himself denoted by the term 'genealogy'; and third, the various semiotic reconstructions of Freudian psychoanalysis developed initially by Jacques Lacan, and further pursued, perhaps even more influentially so, by Julia Kristeva. The ten years after 1974 witnessed the translation into English of a series of key post-structuralist texts. Derrida's *De la grammatologie* and *L'écriture et la différance*, both originally published in 1967, first appeared in English translation in 1974 and 1978 respectively; Barthes's *S/Z* (1970) was first published in English in 1974, *Le plaisir du texte* (1973) in 1975, *Sade, Fourier, Loyola* (1971) in 1976; collections of Foucault's essays dating from 1962 to 1972 and from 1972 to 1977 appeared in English in 1977 and 1980 respectively; 1977 also saw the first English translation of *Surveiller et punir* (1975), 1978 that of the first volume of the *Histoire de la sexualité* (1976); selections from Lacan's 1966 collection of *Écrits* appeared in English in 1977, Kristeva's *La Révolution du langage poétique* (1974) in 1984. Whatever their respective theoretical merits and demerits, there can be little doubt that, in France itself, these three points of departure from structuralism had each borne the dual impress of, first, the initial political disillusionments of the immediate post-1968 period, and second, and latterly, an emergent political conservatism within the French intelligentsia.

For much of the British intelligentsia, however, as also for the Australian, it was Althusserianism which had provided the initial introduction not only to Marxism but also to structuralism, and to what would eventually become significantly post-structuralist thematics. Althusserianism thus established a continuing identification between structuralist theory and radical politics, which would later secure a disproportionately leftist audience for the subsequent importations of French post-structuralism proper. Moreover, the conservative intellectual establishment in Britain, and the literary establishment in particular, sustained until well into the 1980s an implacable hostility to 'structuralism', a term which came to signify not only structuralism proper but also the various post-structuralist successor doctrines, and indeed, all manner of alien 'isms'. The most publicly visible result of this hostility was the so-called 'structuralist controversy' at Cambridge which claimed Colin MacCabe as its victim late in 1981, and also, astonishingly, resulted in the English Faculty's decision to remove its two most distinguished members, Williams himself and Frank Kermode, from its appointments committee. Neither were in any obvious sense 'structuralists'. Indeed, Williams's own response to literary structuralism had been highly sceptical, as he himself recalled: 'When this tendency . . . appeared as an import from France in the sixties, I even risked saying that it seemed strange only because it was a long-lost cousin who had emigrated from Cambridge in the late twenties and early thirties' (Williams, 1984b:206). But both Williams and Kermode had attempted to engage in some sort of productive encounter with contemporary French theory, thereby ensuring the animosity of much mainstream English 'thought' (cf. MacCabe, 1985:17–31). During the late 1970s and the early 1980s, Williams's cultural materialism thus evolved within an intellectual and political milieu which clearly overlapped with that of a certain kind of 'deconstruction'. This was certainly not deconstruction as it was then developing in North America, most especially at Yale (Hartman, 1979), nor even exactly as pursued by Derrida himself. It was, as Anthony Easthope points out, a post-structuralism much more indebted to Marxism in general, and to Althusserianism in particular, than that available either in France or in the United States (Easthope, 1991:21–2, 161–4). Despite a considerable initial antipathy, Williams himself clearly recognised a developing affinity between his own cultural materialism and this kind of 'radical semiotics' (Williams, 1984b:210). Such interpenetrations and interconnections, between cultural materialism, structuralism and post-structuralism, and between each of these and the continuing legacies of more traditional Marxisms and culturalisms, would powerfully shape the development of both cultural studies and literary studies, as also that of the more general intellectual culture of the left.

Cultural Studies

Leavisite literary criticism had constructed popular culture, not as part of the subject matter of 'English' but rather as the discipline's excluded antithetical other. The sheer volume of attention paid popular culture by both Hoggart and Williams, quite apart from the often positive valorisations attached thereto, clearly transgressed those disciplinary boundaries. But whatever Williams's and Hoggart's own personal intentions, English itself proved quite unamenable to the kind of disciplinary reconstruction implied by *The Uses of Literacy* and *The Long Revolution*. Almost by default, then, 'the popular' became the subject matter of the new proto-discipline of 'cultural studies'. In 1962, Hoggart was appointed Professor of Modern English Literature at Birmingham University. Two years later, largely at his instigation, the university established a Centre for Contemporary Cultural Studies, with Hoggart himself as its first director. When Hoggart left to take up a position with UNESCO in 1968, he was succeeded by Stuart Hall. From the very beginning, Hoggart had acknowledged Williams's 'interesting work' in *Culture and Society* as a source of intellectual inspiration (Hoggart, 1970:255). Subsequent commentary has continued to emphasise that the new sub-discipline owed its initial theoretical foundations at least as much to Williams as to Hoggart (Green, 1978:211; Hall, 1980c:58; Jones, 1982:111). Certainly, Williams himself regarded the Centre as 'an excellent pioneering example' (Williams, 1976b:149) of needed institutional innovation. During Hall's term of office, moreover, the Centre became, in effect, the intellectually pre-eminent institutional location for cultural studies, not only in Britain but throughout much of the English-speaking world. As Lawrence Grossberg, from the University of Illinois, observed in his 1988 Power Foundation lecture in Sydney, 'there remains something like a center—to be precise, the tradition of British cultural studies, especially the work of the Centre for Contemporary Cultural Studies' (Grossberg et al., 1988:8). Graeme Turner, a founding editor of the *Australian Journal of Cultural Studies* and a key figure in the development of cultural studies at the University of Queensland, put it even more succinctly: 'the Birmingham Centre . . . can justifiably claim to be the key institution in the history of the field' (Turner, 1990:76).

As director, Hall displayed a remarkable flair for academic entrepreneurship. He established a house journal for the Centre, *Working Papers in Cultural Studies*, eleven issues of which were published during the 1970s. The 1975 double issue, Nos 7/8, and the 1977 issue, No. 10, were each republished in book form by

Hutchinson (Hall and Jefferson, 1976; Centre for Contemporary Cultural Studies, 1978), as was a subsequent retrospective overview of the Centre's work during the period of Hall's directorship (Hall et al., 1980). All three volumes included contributions by Hall himself. In 1978 Hall co-authored, with a number of colleagues from the Birmingham Centre, a highly acclaimed 'cultural studies' account of 'mugging', which sought to analyse the ways in which media constructions of black criminality had functioned so as to confer popular legitimacy on a developing state authoritarianism (Hall et al., 1978a). Though Hall moved from Birmingham in 1979, to take up the chair of sociology at the Open University, his influence over the Centre's intellectual evolution had proved decisive. At the Open University, moreover, he was involved in the co-production of U203, 'Popular Culture', an interdisciplinary undergraduate course, convened by Tony Bennett, now at Griffith University in Brisbane, which ran from 1982 to 1987, and which in its first year attracted over a thousand students (Bennett et al., 1986a:vii). As Easthope observes, U203 was 'the most ambitious, serious and comprehensive intervention in cultural studies in Britain, and, apart from the work of the Birmingham Centre, the most important' (Easthope, 1991:74). The course generated three commercially published, edited collections (Bennett et al., 1981; 1986; Waites et al., 1982), two of which included important essays by Hall (1981; 1986).

More than any other single figure, then, Hall can claim credit for the successful institutionalisation of academic cultural studies in Britain. There is, no doubt, an unavoidable reductionism about any attempt to construct a particular career as fully representative of a collective intellectual project: the Birmingham Centre has had two distinguished directors since Hall, Richard Johnson and Jorge Lorrain; even under Hall's directorship it produced work much less clearly marked by his direct influence (Women's Studies Group, 1978; Clarke et al., 1979); and there have been 'centres' other than Birmingham, for example, the Centre for Cultural Studies at Leeds University and the Centre for Mass Communication Research at Leicester, or, in Australia, the Institute for Cultural Policy Studies at Griffith. But for all this necessary qualification, Hall's career does in fact enjoy an unusually representative quality, sufficiently so at least to justify an initial approach to the question of the relationship between cultural studies and cultural materialism by way of an examination of that between his work and that of Williams. Williams and Hall had worked together on the founding, Old New Left, editorial board of the *New Left Review*; they had co-authored with Thompson the Old New Left's major political manifesto (Hall et al., 1968); and as Hall himself would later recall, 'we have found ourselves shaping up to the same issues, or crises: and shaping up . . . from the same directions' (Hall, 1989:54). These affinities were not merely political. As Easthope observes: 'Cultural studies, media studies, work on television and film, the teaching of communication—all these in Britain bear the imprint of the work of Raymond Williams. That work has been widely promoted by the Birmingham Centre . . . led . . . by Stuart Hall' (Easthope, 1991:71). There is an element of exaggeration here: the Centre's commitment to ethnographic research, for example, clearly owes more to Hoggart than to Williams. But it is certainly true that, for much of the 1970s at least, there was an unusually close parallelism between Williams's and Hall's respective intellectual evolutions: both very clearly moved from an essentially left-Leavisite culturalism toward a more properly Gramscian perspective. The 'concept of "hegemony"', Hall would recall in 1980, 'has played a seminal role in Cultural Studies' (Hall, 1980a:35). And as late as 1976, Hall and his colleagues in the Centre had paired the concept of hegemony with that of culture, in ways which simultaneously echoed the argument of Williams's 1973 'Base and Superstructure' essay and anticipated that of *Marxism and Literature* itself (Clarke et al., 1976:10–13).

Hall, however, had proved much more responsive than Williams to the lure both of Althusserianism in particular and of structuralism in general. Indeed, Hall's essay 'Encoding and Decoding in Television Discourse', originally published as a CCCS Stencilled Paper as early as 1973, had drawn heavily on French and Italian semiotic theory so as to mount a very effective critique of American mass-communications theory (Hall, 1980b). More pointedly, the Centre's 1978 volume, *On Ideology*, chose to situate Gramsci in relation to Althusser rather than to Williams; and what is true of the volume as a whole is true also of Hall's own particular contributions (1978a; Hall et al., 1978b). The precise point at which these divergences finally come to constitute a difference is difficult to document. By 1980, however, when Hall first published his seminal sketch of the current state of the theoretical art in cultural studies (1980c), Williams's 'culturalism' was no longer the obviously available starting point for the would-be discipline, but rather only one of two competing paradigms, each with its attendant strengths and weaknesses. This essay, 'Cultural studies: two paradigms', was included as a set text for U203; it was republished in one of the Open University readers (Bennett et al., 1981:19–37), and again in a later collection of articles from *Media, Culture and Society* (Collins et al., 1986:33–48), and it soon came to provide a central organising device for theoretical debate in the field. It rehearses much that had previously been argued by Richard Johnson, including, of course, the distinction itself between 'culturalism' and 'structuralism' (Johnson, 1979), but is nonetheless much more preoccupied with the theoretical status of Williams's own work. Furthermore, it was published very nearly simultaneously with an extended commentary by Hall on the *Politics and Letters* collection of interviews with Williams (Hall, 1980d). This latter was to be included in Eagleton's 1989 *Festschrift*, and might thus be considered fairly close to Hall's last word on the subject of Williams's influence. Together, the two pieces provide a fairly concise statement of Hall's reactions not only to Williams's earlier left culturalism but also to his mature cultural materialism.

Hall himself actually registers no such distinction in Williams's work, but rather 'a striking continuity of basic position . . . even in his more acceptable recent formulations' (Hall, 1989:62). In the 'Cultural studies: two paradigms' essay, at least, Williams's work is also closely identified with that of Thompson, as parallel instances of a similar culturalism: the continuity runs not only between *Culture and Society* and *The Making of the English Working Class*, but also, and much more surprisingly, between *Marxism and Literature* and *The Poverty of Theory*. For Hall, the concept of 'culture' in Williams and that of 'experience' in Thompson perform fundamentally analogous theoretical functions, that is, they denote simultaneously, and thereby elide the distinction between, active consciousness on the one hand, and relatively 'given', determinate conditions on the other. The result is a theoretical humanism, with two distinguishing characteristics: first, a general 'experiential pull', and second, an 'emphasis on the creative' (Hall, 1980c:63). For both

Thompson and Williams, then, the 'authenticating position' (ibid.), or 'authenticating test' (Hall, 1989:62), is, in Hall's view, that provided by 'experience'. Hall's response to such empiricism is almost conventionally structuralist:

> Analysis must deconstruct . . . 'lived wholeness' in order to be able to think its determinate conditions . . . This confusion, which persists even in Williams's later work . . . continues to have disabling theoretical effects . . . So long as 'experience' continues to play this all-embracing role, there will be an inevitable theoretical pull towards reading all structures as if they expressively correlated with one another. (ibid.)

The scene is set, then, for the structuralist 'interruption' as theoretical salvation. And so it emerges: structuralism recognises the presence of constraining relations of structure; it acknowledges the importance of different levels of theoretical abstraction; it conceives of the social whole as an adequately complex unity-in-difference; it successfully replaces the category of experience with that of ideology (Hall, 1980c:67–9). Formally, of course, Hall aspires not to any thoroughgoing structuralism but to a Gramscian synthesis of the two paradigms: 'between them . . . they address what must be the *core problem* of Cultural Studies' (ibid.:72). The developmental logic of the argument, however, actually leaves culturalism with remarkably little to do. Its strengths, we learn, 'can almost be derived from the weaknesses of the structuralist position' (ibid.:69), which is surely as backhanded a compliment as they come; and these belong, in any case, quite specifically to Gramsci rather than to Williams or to Thompson. In truth, Hall's is an anti-culturalist argument, its effects all the more damaging both for its professed evenhandedness and for the quasi-filial respect it accords the 'culturalists': to become a 'founding father' is to become, perhaps unavoidably, just a little passé.

To some extent, Hall caricatures both Williams and Thompson. Neither is quite so unaware of structural determinacy as Hall suggests: indeed, Williams's notion of determination as the setting of limits and exertion of pressures, though certainly not structuralist, is nonetheless fully compatible with a strong sense of structure. Nor are they quite so empiricist: Williams's own work is in many respects intensely theoretical, as Hall himself has had cause to remark (Hall, 1980a:19); and, the title of Thompson's *The Poverty of Theory* not withstanding, its argument actually develops a highly nuanced account of the dialogue between theory and evidence in historical research (Thompson, 1978:197–242). And, if Williams prefers the concept of hegemony to that of ideology, this is for reasons that are both theoretically articulate in their own right and theoretically defensible in terms of a broadly 'Gramscian' aproach to cultural analysis. The point, however, is that Hall's Gramsci derives not so much from Williams as from Ernesto Laclau and Chantal Mouffe (Laclau, 1977; Mouffe, 1979; Laclau and Mouffe, 1988). The difference between these respective readings of Gramsci takes us to what is actually the theoretical heart of the matter: that of whether to understand hegemony as culture or as structure, and of what relative weights to attach to the hegemonic and counter-hegemonic respectively. If hegemony is a culture, then it is materially produced by the practices of conscious agents, and may be countered by alternative, counter-hegemonic, practices; if hegemony is a structure of ideology, then it will determine the subjectivity of its subjects in ways which radically diminish the prospects for counter-hegemonic practice, except in the characterisically attenuated form of a plurality of post-structuralist resistant readings. Hegemony as culture is a matter of material production, reproduction and consumption; hegemony as structure is a matter for textual decoding. Where Williams's interpretation of Gramsci's work remains resolutely 'post-culturalist', Hall progressively assimilates it to a developing structuralist—and post-structuralist—paradigm. Hence, for example, Hall's eventual view of Gramsci as anticipating 'many of the actual advances in theorizing' brought about by 'structuralism, discourse and linguistic theory or psychoanalysis' (Hall, 1988a:56).

These theoretical differences increasingly devolve, moreover, on to a particular substantive issue, that of 'Thatcherism'. This is the term used by Hall to refer to the radical right political project pursued by the British Conservative Party under the leadership of Margaret Thatcher, initially in opposition and later in government, in the late 1970s and the 1980s. During this period the Conservatives won three successive general elections and presided over a substantial restructuring, both of the British economy toward privatisation and away from socialisation, and of the British state toward neo-liberalism and away from social-democratic corporatism. In *Policing the Crisis*, the Birmingham Centre had sought to produce a cultural studies account of phenomena more conventionally deemed political, sociological or criminological. From 1979 on, Hall engaged in a theoretically analogous attempt to analyse the more general and more expressly political phenomenon of Thatcherite Toryism. The issues at stake belong to cultural studies, nonetheless, rather than, say, political science, in so far as they pertain to the social construction of consent: 'What is particularly significant for our purposes', writes Hall, 'is Thatcherism's capacity to become popular, especially among those sectors of society whose interests it cannot possibly be said to represent in any conventional sense of the term' (ibid.:41). Hall's analysis begins with the assumption that Thatcherism is substantially different from earlier forms of Conservatism, and that this difference centres on the particular ways in which hegemony is established and maintained. What is at issue, Hall argues, is the 'move toward "authoritarian populism"—an exceptional form of the capitalist state which . . . has been able to construct around itself an active popular consent' (Hall, 1983:22–3). Hall proceeds thence to his central contention, that such consent has been secured by the effective articulation of Thatcherism with certain key elements in traditional working–class culture: 'these discourses operated directly on popular elements in the traditional philosophies and practical ideologies of the *dominated* classes' (ibid.:30). This is possible because such elements 'have no intrinsic, necessary or fixed class meaning' and can therefore be recomposed in new ways, so as 'to construct the people into a populist political subject: *with*, not against, the power bloc' (ibid.). A structuralist understanding of discourse as necessarily 'polysemic' is thus combined, in Hall's account, with an equally structuralist sense of popular passivity, so as to 'construct' much of the British working class itself as positively Thatcherite.

Unsurprisingly, the substantive analysis appeared to Williams even more wrongheaded than the theoretical. Thus the scale of Conservative electoral victory seemed to him much more readily explicable in terms of the peculiar, 'first-past-the-post' British electoral system than of any successfully Thatcherite ideological mobilisation (Williams, 1989b:163). In *Towards 2000*, moreover, Williams shows very clearly that pro-Labour loyalties persist among union members, the unemployed, and manual workers (Williams, 1983:156–7); and that the fall in the Labour vote was as much a consequence of the recent split in the party as of any direct transfer to the Conservatives (ibid.:155). But Williams's objections are fundamentally neither empirical nor empiricist. They are fuelled, rather, by his dual sense of the importance of creative human agency, and of himself as an 'organic' working–class intellectual (Jones, 1982:113), bound to his class of origin by ties of community and kinship, solidarity and 'loyalties' (Williams, 1985). It is simply unthinkable for Williams that the working class should prove as susceptible to bourgeois hegemony as Hall appears to believe possible. That Hall can so readily think the unthinkable is not necessarily, of course, a sign of strength, though he often seems to imply as much (Hall, 1988b:20). Certainly, their predictably different responses to the 1984–5 British coalminers' strike inspire something less than complete confidence in Hall's political judgement. At the height of the strike, in September 1984, Hall seriously argued, in the columns of the Labour Party journal, *New Socialist,* that the Labour-run, and soon to be abolished, Greater London Council had 'become the most important front in the struggle against Thatcherism' (Hall, 1984:37). Williams's own reactions were very different: 'The point of growth for a reviving socialism', he wrote in an article originally published in the same journal, 'is now in all these crisis-ridden communities . . . It is here . . . that new popular forces are forming and looking for some effective political articulation . . . The miners have, in seeking to protect their own interests, outlined a new form of the general interest' (Williams, 1989b:127).

In the early 1980s, then, the major theoretical differences between Williams and Hall, and between cultural materialism and cultural studies, had revolved around their respectively culturalist and structuralist appropriations of Gramsci. But, as the decade proceeded, post-structuralist thematics, particularly those deriving from Foucault, became much more obviously present in cultural studies, both in Britain and in Australia. Hall's later writings on Thatcherism, for example, clearly owe something to this Foucauldian influence (Hall, 1988a:51–3). A more developed Foucauldianism appears in Australia, however, especially in the work of the Institute for Cultural

Policy Studies at Griffith University. The key figure here is almost certainly Tony Bennett, the former chairman of the Open University's U203 course, who became the Institute's first director in 1987. Like Hall at Birmingham, Bennett displayed a considerable flair for academic entrepreneurship: the Institute published a series of *Occasional Papers*, it organised conferences, engaged in extensive, commissioned research on cultural policy, and from 1989 onwards maintained a regular house journal, *Culture and Policy*. Cultural policy studies was clearly envisaged as a quite distinctive politico-cultural project both by Bennett himself and by his co-workers: most obviously Ian Hunter, whose celebrated *Culture and Government* had sought to analyse popular literary education as productive of 'an ethical technology directed to forming the moral attributes of a citizenry' (Hunter, 1988:152); and Colin Mercer, another veteran of U203, who would succeed to the Institute's directorship in 1991. Partly at their instigation, the first two conferences of the Australian Cultural Studies Association were often radically polarised around the merits and demerits of policy studies.

This shift toward cultural policy was never simply pragmatic, but rather evolved from out of a very particular vision of the role of the intellectual, and a correspondingly particular version of cultural politics, both of which derived in essence from Foucault. Foucault's genealogy had sought to relativise discourse, not by any radical reconstruction of the notion of signification, such as is attempted by Derrida, but by the attempt to substitute relations of power for relations of meaning. For Foucault, power in modern society had become essentially ubiquitous and, in its ubiquity, open and indeterminate, productive rather than simply oppressive: 'it induces pleasure, forms knowledge, produces discourse', he writes: 'It needs to be considered as a productive network which runs through the whole social body' (Foucault, 1980:119). There is, then, no single structure of power, but rather a play of powers; and no possibility of an objectively structuralist account of discourse, but only that of a strategic, or tactical, intervention into this play. The proper political function of the intellectual can, therefore, no longer be that of the Sartrean 'universal intellectual', who acts as 'the consciousness/conscience of us all', but must become that of the 'specific intellectual', who will work 'within specific sectors, at the precise points where their own conditions of life or work situate them' (ibid.:126). If Williams's role in cultural theory can perhaps be considered Sartrean (*The Times* did, after all, describe him as a British equivalent to Sartre), then Bennett's, by contrast, is determinedly 'specific'.

The underlying theoretical rationale behind Bennett's own commitment to cultural policy studies is most clearly articulated in his *Outside Literature*, the original title of which, interestingly enough, was planned to be *Against Literature* (Bennett, 1985:49). In a reversal of Williams's intellectual journey towards Marxism, Bennett here sets out to exorcise the ghosts of his own misspent Marxist youth (cf. Bennett, 1979). For Bennett, 'it no longer seems . . . fruitful to regard Marxism as . . . adequate to the theorisation of social phenomena' (Bennett, 1990:7). Marxism's central failure in the field of cultural studies has been, in Bennett's view, its enduring loyalty to the 'idealist concerns of bourgeois aesthetics' (ibid.:33). To such idealism he seeks to counterpose a thoroughgoing 'cultural materialism', though one which derives much more obviously from Foucault than from Williams. Bennett's argument commences from a general critique of the base/superstructure model, in which he proposes an alternatively 'sociological' understanding of literary relations as in themselves social relations. At first sight this seems little more than a restatement of Williams's own position. But there are at least two alternative routes by which to sidestep the dualism between base and supestructure, 'real' history and 'less real' literature: either, like Williams, one chooses to historicise literature; or, like Foucault and Derrida, one chooses to narrativise history. Bennett clearly opts for the latter: history, he argues, 'is most appropriately regarded as a specific discursive regime . . . through which the maintenance/ transformation of the past as a set of currently existing realities is regulated' (ibid.:50).

History thus disposed of, Bennett proceeds to a critique of Marxist aesthetics as little more than a re-run of bourgeois 'philosophical aesthetics'. Here the argument begins from premises very similar to Williams's own deconstruction of 'the aesthetic' in *Marxism and Literature*. Philosophical aesthetics misconstrue literary and artistic judgement as universal modes of cognition, Bennett argues, rather than as socially specific applications of the particular rules of value shared by particular valuing communities. They thereby 'fetishise the objects of value and deploy a discourse of disqualification in relation to those subjects who do not . . . conform to their edicts' (ibid.:160). In aesthetic discourse, then, the relative intolerance characteristic of all discourses of value effectively 'becomes absolute' (ibid.:165). Hence Bennett's rejection of all such notions of aesthetic value, whether Leavisite, Marxist or whatever. In so far as aesthetics was ever a discourse of value pure and simple, then Bennett's case against the aesthetic seems virtually unassailable. But there had invariably been more than this to aesthetics, as Williams himself clearly demonstrated in *Culture and Society*, and as Terry Eagleton has reiterated in his recent *The Ideology of the Aesthetic* (1990). In any case, Bennett's critique of the aesthetic proceeds very quickly to a critique of criticism itself, which radically calls into question not only more conventionally Marxist versions of critical practice but also, if only by implication, Williams's own. Bennett's argument is that such recent Marxist and quasi-Marxist critics as Eagleton, Edward Said, Fredric Jameson and Frank Lentricchia, each in effect replicate an original Arnoldian, and later Leavisite, sense of the proper 'function of criticism'. Such Marxisms have tended, he writes, 'to re-align criticism with a totalising conception of social and cultural critique' (ibid.:194). They aspire to secure a political relevance for criticism only 'by going back to being what it once was—a set of interpretive procedures oriented towards the transformation of the conscious-ness of individual subjects' (ibid.:195). This is, of course, the established function of Foucault's 'universal intellectual'. In Bennett's view, following Foucault, such criticisms 'reflect a fundamental failure to pose questions of literary politics in ways that are sufficiently precise and focused to make a sustained difference to the functioning of literary institutions' (ibid.:286). For Bennett himself, by contrast, the Foucauldian notion of the 'specific intellectual' de-mands 'more specific and localised assessments of the effects of practices of textual commentary conducted in the light of the institutionally circumscribed fields of their social deployment' (ibid.:10). Rather than denounce the world, Bennett will reform the university— and as much else of the culture industries as seems practically reformable.

There is some limited overlap between Bennett's position here and that deployed in *Marxism and Literature*, and again in *Keywords*, where Williams indicts criticism as 'ideological', on the grounds that it 'actively prevents that understanding of response which does not assume the habit (or right or duty) of judgement' (Williams, 1976a:76). Both Bennett and Williams envisage criticism's supersession by a kind of literary and cultural studies that will be essentially sociological in character. Their respective understandings of sociality itself nonetheless point towards very different kinds of cultural sociology. As Williams makes clear in the *Politics and Letters* interviews, his own objections to criticism are levelled not so much at judgement per se, which seems to him 'inevitable', but at the 'pseudo-impersonality' of literary-critical judgement in particular (Williams, 1979a:334–6). Indeed, his generally humanist reading of the importance of social agency and of social consciousness, as also his continuing sense of class loyalty, actually require non-specialist value–judgements of a more or less explicit kind. For if the long revolution is to be continued, then everyday arguments, about culture and society, politics and letters, must succeed in changing people's minds, that is, in the 'transformation of the consciousness of individual subjects': there is quite simply no other way to proceed for a politics that will not only be democratic but also inspired, as it were, 'from below'. For Bennett, by contrast, a 'specific intelligentsia' can effectively prosecute an essentially technocratic micropolitics 'from above'. Cultural policy studies thus stands in relation to cultural studies itself much as Fabian social engineering once did to sociology. Bennett aspires, in short, to examine 'the truth/power symbiosis which characterises particular regions of social management—with a view not only to undoing that symbiosis but also . . . installing a new one in its place' (Bennett, 1990:270).

Both Bennett and Hall owe a very clear debt to Williams, which both appear happy to acknowledge (Bennett, 1989:86–7; Hall, 1989:55). But, equally clearly, in response to structuralism and post-structuralism they each move away from Williams, though in rather different directions. For Hall the central, pressing problem becomes that of Thatcherism, for Bennett that of cultural policy. These theoretical differences are in part, at least, a consequence of the very different political circumstances which pertained in Britain and Australia during the 1980s. Bennett's new Fabianism has arisen in conditions as specific and particular as those which provoked Hall to the diagnosis of 'authoritarian populism': during the 1980s, while British Labour languished in opposition, the Australian Labor Party won four successive federal elections. Had Australian cultural studies been an essentially 'right-wing' discourse, as Leavisite English undoubtedly was, or for that matter as neo-classical economics undoubtedly is, then we might well have witnessed much Australian intellectual anguish about 'Hawkism', or perhaps even 'authoritarian corporatism'. And had the British Labour Party won four successive general elections, then Birmingham too might have tried its hand at 'cultural engineering'. These counterfactual examples suggest something rather interesting, that is, the extent to which these developments in academic cultural theory actually depend upon quite contingent politico-cultural 'conjunctures'.

In *The Politics of Modernism*, Williams asks exasperatedly of cultural theory: 'Is there never to be an end to petit-bourgeois theorists making long-term adjustments to short-term situations?' (Williams, 1989a:175). I doubt that he actually had Bennett in mind here at all, though the immediately preceding reference to a 'block diagnosis of Thatcherism which taught despair and political disarmament' (ibid.) might well be read as pointing toward Hall. Clearly, however, both Bennett and Hall were deeply implicated in the theoretical moment of structuralism, which Williams's polemic here takes as its target. Moreover, these more general objections to structuralism are at one point quite specifically directed at both cultural studies and the Open University (ibid.:157). Whatever Williams's immediate intentions, we do indeed find, in both Bennett and Hall, precisely such long-term adjustments to short-term situations. I suspect that sober retrospective analysis will eventually show that Thatcherite Toryism impinged much less on British popular consciousness than Hall has sought to argue; but also that much less was achieved by way of cultural renovation under Australian Labor, even at the micropolitical level, than Bennett appeared to believe possible. A thoroughgoing cultural materialism such as Williams established, which acknowledges the claims of agency *and* structure as neither structuralisms nor post-structuralisms have been able to do, might well have spared cultural studies this particular set of embarrassments.

Much closer to Williams's later work is the kind of cultural and media studies associated with Nicholas Garnham and his colleagues and former colleagues in Communication Studies at the University of Westminister, formerly the Polytechnic of Central London. Garnham himself is Professor of Media Studies and Director of the Centre for Communication and Information Studies at Westminister, author of *Capitalism and Communication* (1990) and co-author of *The Economics of Television* (Collins et al., 1988); James Curran, who moved from PCL in 1985 to head the Department of Communications at Goldsmiths' College in the University of London, is the co-author of *Power Without Responsibility* (Curran and Seaton, 1981), a highly acclaimed history of British press and broadcasting, informed theoretically by a culturalist reading of Gramsci, and co-editor of *Mass Communication and Society*, a very widely used media studies textbook (Curran et al., 1977). Both were founding editors in 1979 of the PCL house journal *Media, Culture and Society*, which from its very beginning had included Williams, Hoggart and also Pierre Bourdieu in its editorial advisory board. The journal's opening manifesto, written by Curran, sought to place it in relation to an intellectual environment dominated, on the left, by the kind of theoreticist structural Marxism increasingly associated with Hall, Birmingham, and the Open University, and, on 'the right', by essentially empiricist studies of 'media effects'. The new journal, Curran promised, would favour neither orthodoxy, but would 'encourage research and debate within and between these two traditions' (Curran, 1979:2). In retrospect, this appears more than a little disingenuous. As its editors would concede in a 1986 retrospective, *Media, Culture and Society* had then still published nothing from the 'media effects' tradition and nor did it intend to do so (Collins et al., 1986a:2). Moreover, they continued, the journal 'was in large measure conceived as a counter-argument' to Althusserian and post-Althusserian structural Marxism (ibid.:4). Its distinctive contribution, they now acknowledged, was a stress, first, on the ways in which culture is produced, and second, on media and communication policy viewed not from a technical or administrative vantage point but from that of a 'critical intelligentsia', serving a 'democratic public interest' (ibid.:4–5). Though there is no explicit reference to

Williams here, this is more or less exactly the project identified in his own later work.

The *Media, Culture and Society* approach has on occasion been represented as little more than a return to economistic Marxism (Turner, 1990:194–5). But this is surely a misrepresentation of a developing position which owes at least as much to cultural materialism as to historical materialism. Even Garnham's most aggressively political-economic critique of the Birmingham tradition, first published in the journal in 1979, actually takes as its theoretical starting point Williams's *Marxism and Literature* (Garnham, 1986:9). Even Colin Sparks, surely the most orthodoxly Marxist of the *Media, Culture and Society* editors, views Williams's work as establishing 'valuable and progressive positions' (Sparks, 1980:134). In the 1979 essay cited above, Garnham had, in fact, expressed some reservation about Williams's position: it 'suffers from a misleading reductionism by failing to distinguish between the material and the economic' (Garnham, 1986:14), he had argued. The criticism seems to me misdirected, for, as we saw in the preceding chapter, Williams in fact made exactly this distinction and indeed made use of it in ways which clearly anticipate Garnham's own interests. In any case, the following year Garnham and Williams were to work closely together on a special issue of *Media, Culture and Society*, intended as an introduction for English-speaking audiences to Bourdieu's sociology of culture (Garnham, 1980; Garnham and Williams, 1986). By 1983, moreover, Garnham was happy to assert a much closer identification between his work and that of Williams. Arguing against both media effects research and structural Marxism as sharing a common idealism, he would insist on the need for a 'major shift in perspective and emphasis', within media and cultural studies, towards 'what is coming to be called . . . cultural materialism' (Garnham, 1983:321). Garnham's stress here on 'the irreducible material determinants of the social process of symbolic exchange' (ibid.), as also on the need for communication scholars 'both as citizens and scholars . . . to decide . . . which side they are on' (ibid.:329), are each deeply reminiscent of Williams. It would be absurd to suggest that every single article in every single issue of *Media, Culture and Society* is somehow directly inspired by Williams. But it most certainly is not absurd to suggest that the journal's continuing project derives direct theoretical inspiration from that stress on cultural production which distinguished *Marxism and Literature* and *Culture*, nor that its substantive focus is very much that defined in *Communications* and *Television: Technology and Cultural Form*. Of the journal's Australian corresponding editors, Lesley Johnson, professor of communications at the University of Western Sydney, has certainly acknowledged a very clear debt to Williams's work (Johnson, 1987:176–7; 1988:4). It is in such studies of the institutional production of culture, rather than in decodings of cultural texts or in technocratic cultural policy studies, that Williams's central theoretical legacy seems to me the more powerfully present.

Literary Studies

We have taken as our main focus in this chapter cultural and media studies, rather than literary studies, for the very good reason that the entire direction of Williams's effort points toward a radical decentring of 'Literature', and its eventual supersession into a more general cultural sociology. As Jonathan Dollimore, a self-proclaimed cultural materialist, but also a lecturer in English, rightly observes, theory such as this makes possible 'a truly interdisciplinary approach to—some might say exit from—the subject' (Dollimore, 1985:2). That said, we do need to note both that much of Williams's work was indeed conducted within literary studies and drama studies, and that his intellectual influence in these areas remains substantial. From the mid–1960s onwards, in literary studies as in cultural studies, the newly imported continental European 'Theory', whether Western Marxist, structuralist or post-structuralist, came into direct and immediate conflict with an already dominant culturalism. But whereas cultural studies itself had been in part the effect of a rupture within culturalism, a rupture clearly marked by *The Uses of Literacy* and *The Long Revolution*, literary studies proper remained very much the domain of a more or less unreconstructed Leavisism. Certainly, Terry Eagleton recalls 'in the early 1960s, a Cambridge which was buzzing with the Leavis argument' (Eagleton, 1985:131). And, according to Kathy MacDermott's analysis of first year university examiners' comments, English studies at the University of Melbourne was dominated by a distinctively Leavisite 'ideologeme' even as late as the early 1970s (MacDermott, 1983:104). If culturalist resistances to Theory were greater in English than elsewhere, so too were the issues at stake, at least in England itself. As has been argued on more than one occasion, the discipline of English studies had been constructed as occupying a peculiarly central location within the English national culture (Anderson, 1970:276; Doyle, 1982:17; Baldick, 1983:95). The nationalism which we noted in chapter two as characteristic of Leavisism was at once both constitutive of and constituted by this centrality. The incursion of Theory, sometimes radical and always foreign, into what had been widely understood as the very heart of the national culture, thus precipitated what Peter Widdowson rightly termed a 'crisis in English studies': 'a question, posed from within, as to what English *is*, where it has got to, whether it has a future, whether it *should* have a future as a discrete discipline, and if it does, in what ways it might be reconstituted' (Widdowson, 1982:7). Williams's cultural materialism had been one of a number of theoretical positions, and the only one truly from within the discipline, which had decisively contributed to the formulation of precisely such questions as these.

The crisis was acted out in a number of different institutional and discursive spaces: in the 'Sociology of Literature' conferences organised annually from 1976 to 1984, by Francis Barker and his colleagues from the Department of Literature at Essex University; in the journal *Literature and History*, edited, in its first incarnation from 1975 to 1988, by Widdowson and others in the School of Humanities at Thames Polytechnic; in the more specifically literary interventions of socialist or feminist journals such as the *New Left Review* or *Feminist Review*; and, at least as a source of theoretical provocation, in the film studies journal *Screen*. At a slightly later date, a self-proclaimed 'third generation' of radical literary theorists would coalesce around Oxford English Limited and the journal *News From Nowhere*. If the crisis begins with that rupture within culturalism, from out of which cultural studies emerged, then it proceeds thereafter through three reasonably well defined stages. In the first, the radical critique is overwhelmingly Marxist in character, its own internal debates in effect a confrontation between culturalist and structuralist Marxisms, represented respectively by Williams and Althusser. This is the point at which both *Literature and History* and the Essex conferences were launched; the point at which Stuart Hall could affirm, in his opening contribution to the first such conference, that 'every one of these developments has, in some way or another, been generated by Marxism' (Hall, 1976:5). Williams's own position, poised somewhere between an earlier left culturalism and a not quite fully realised cultural materialism, still remained actively in play with these other, more explicitly Althusserian Marxisms, best represented in literary studies, of course, by his own former student, Terry Eagleton. Williams himself presented to the second Essex conference a paper which deployed his own theoretical distinction between dominant, residual and emergent cultural elements with some panache (Williams, 1977b). He was from the beginning an editorial adviser to *Literature and History*, though, unlike Eagleton, never actually a contributor. He wrote regularly for the *New Left Review*, though the journal's increasingly Althusserian tenor must then have seemed better suited to Eagleton's work. In the second stage, during the late 1970s and early 1980s, we witness an interesting reversal, by which Williams's own work had now become more declaredly Marxist, while at much the same time Althusserian structuralism had imploded in on itself, leaving behind a legacy of variously Derridean, Foucauldian and Lacanian post-structuralisms. This is the theoretical moment of *Screen* and the occasion for Williams' development of cultural materialism, from *Marxism and Literature* through to *Culture*. This is also the political moment of a kind of radical feminism, often determinedly post-structuralist in its theoretical predilections, to which Williams would respond with some difficulty.

The third and final stage is that from the early to mid–1980s onwards, in which Williams's work seems to attract an increasing audience both among erstwhile Althusserian recidivists, including Eagleton himself, and among the still younger generation of scholars represented by Oxford English Limited. As the latter group would affirm shortly after Williams's death: 'The whole project of Oxford English Limited from its inception owed much to Williams . . . with Williams dead, who is there now to send one's books to?' (Oxford English Limited, 1989:10). This last stage entails more than mere piety toward a 'grand old man of the left', though there was certainly some of that, for example, in press commentary on Williams's political role within the Socialist Society, from 1982 on. It represents, rather, a serious theoretical shift towards a recognisable cultural materialism. In his introduction to a 1985 collection of *New Essays in Cultural Materialism*, Dollimore (1985:15) cites as instances of such work not only Williams himself but also Terry Lovell (1980), Janet Wolff (1981), his own co-editor, Alan Sinfield (1983), and the Terry Eagleton of *Literary Theory* (1983). Both Lovell and Wolff have continued to combine a broadly cultural materialist theoretical position with distinctly feminist politics (Lovell, 1987:5; Wolff, 1990:5). As for Eagleton, something close to his final judgement must be that written for the 1989 *Critical Perspectives* volume: 'Williams . . . refused to be distracted by the wilder flights of Althusserian or post-structuralist theory and was still there, ready and waiting for us, when some of us younger theorists, sadder and wiser, finally re-emerged from one or two cul-de-sacs to rejoin him where we had left off' (Eagleton, 1989b:6). Sinfield's later work certainly does take issue with the alleged universalism of Williams's 'left-culturalism' (Sinfield, 1989:242–3, 300), but it does so, nonetheless, precisely on the grounds of a whole set of cultural–materialist categories: cultural production, the distinction between dominant, residual and emergent practices, 'middle class dissidence', and so on (ibid.:26–7, 31, 35). One could continue with many other examples; the most recent that comes to hand is Christopher Hampton's *The Ideology of the Text* (Hampton, 1990:151–73). Despite Greenfield and Williams's optimism (Greenfield and Williams, 1989:137), specifically Australian examples are less readily available: perhaps we need to await Peter Williams's own full-length study of Frank Hardy.

Anthony Easthope distinguishes two main currents in what he terms British 'post-structuralist' literary theory (Easthope, 1991:153): first, that kind of textual 'deconstruction', pursued by MacCabe and by Catherine Belsey (1980), which sought to analyse the ways in which the text makes available to the reader certain definable subject positions; and second, the kind of 'institutional' analysis, pursued most notably by the later Eagleton but also by Tony Bennett, which sought to problematise the institutional conditions of the production of textual meaning. The latter is what Easthope means by 'left deconstruction' (ibid.). These are what Howard Felperin refers to as 'textualist' and 'contextualist' versions of post-structuralism, which he associates, respectively, with the work of Derrida and Foucault

(Felperin, 1985:71–2). Felperin's formulation seems appropriate both to the Australian and the American intellectual contexts: textualist deconstruction, such as his own in Australia or that of the Yale school in the United States, is by and large Derridean; contextualist deconstruction, such as that of John Frow in Australia (Frow, 1986) or Frank Lentricchia in the United States (Lentricchia, 1980), by and large Foucauldian. But, as Easthope rightly stresses, MacCabe and Belsey actually work with a style of deconstruction that derives at least as much from Althusser, by way of *Screen*, as from Derrida (Easthope, 1991:134–5). Where Easthope is mistaken, it seems to me, is to see 'left deconstruction' as essentially Foucauldian, or even as at all 'post-structuralist'. For in Britain this kind of work actually derives its inspiration not from Foucault but from Williams, and is thus not so much post-structuralist as 'post-culturalist'.

The text in which Eagleton, for example, most clearly retreats from his earlier Althusserian structuralism (Eagleton, 1981:97), is precisely that in which he also dismisses the Anglophone reception of Foucault as providing 'a glamorous rationale for erstwhile revolutionaries unnerved into pessimism' (ibid.:58); comments on Derridean deconstruction that 'only a powerless petty-bourgeois intelligentsia would raise it to the solemn dignity of a philosophy' (ibid.:142); but attributes to Williams 'bold efforts to shift attention from the analysis of an object named "literature" to the social relations of cultural practice' (ibid.:97). Bennett's *Formalism and Marxism* is similarly indebted to Williams, rather than to Foucault (Bennett, 1979:13–6); and, in so far as the much later *Outside Literature* is indeed Foucauldian, then, as we have seen, this really does represent a very significant theoretical shift on Bennett's part. Even Easthope credits Williams's 'Base and Superstructure' essay, a text which betrays not the slightest evidence of interest in Foucault, as the original source for left deconstruction in Britain (ibid.:14). No doubt there are, as Dollimore has stressed, certain very clear affinities between British cultural materialism and that kind of North American Foucauldian criticism which has come to be known as the 'new historicism' (Dollimore, 1985:3). But it is simply perverse for Easthope, writing in an expressly British context, to attempt to reduce the former to the latter. He is right, nonetheless, to contrast the line running from Williams with that from Althusser, through *Screen*. From 1971, when its editorial board was reconstructed around Sam Rohdie, *Screen*, the journal of the Society for Education in Film and Television (SEFT), became the effective intellectual centre, or perhaps 'decentre', initially for 'cultural' Althusserianism, later for textualist post-structuralism. Its influence extended well beyond the specialist area of film studies and, through MacCabe, as we noted earlier, even into Cambridge English studies.

MacCabe's training was in English and his own work would include not only cinema studies but also an intellectually provocative study of James Joyce (MacCabe, 1978). Theoretically, MacCabe's work aspired to analyse the ways in which different kinds of text differently position their readers: the revolutionary implications of Joyce's writing are thus in the way it 'produces a change in the relations between reader and text' (ibid.:1). Substantively, this led to a sustained assault on literary and cinematic 'realism', which threatened no less than a dramatic reversal of the conventional polarities of pre-existing cultural radicalisms. Both orthodoxly Communist Marxism and Lukácsian 'critical' Marxism (Lukács, 1963) had typically privileged literary realism as against 'bourgeois' modernism. Moreover, quite apart from Communist dogma, many radical writers and film-makers had strongly believed in the potentially subversive effect of realistic technique: by virtue of its capacity to expose to public view previously hidden aspects of contemporary social reality, realism, it was believed, would quite literally 'raise the consciousness' of its audiences. But French post-structuralism had developed a powerful critique of such literary realisms, deriving, in the first place, from Barthes's distinction between readerly and writerly texts, that is, respectively, those which position the reader as passive consumer and those which demand that the reader actively participate as co-author of the text (Barthes, 1974:4). In somewhat analogous terms, MacCabe would argue that 'the classic realist text' is one which positions the reading subject in what he calls a 'relation of dominant specularity', that is, in terms of a relationship between the subject and the real, in which the real 'is not articulated—it is' (MacCabe, 1985:39). The structure of the classic realist text, MacCabe argues, is to be found both in the bourgeois novel and in film, and it is one which, ironically, 'cannot deal with the real in its contradiction because of the unquestioned status of the representation at the level of the dominant discourse' (ibid.). Echoing Barthes and invoking Brecht (Brecht, 1980), in direct defiance of the Lukácsian tradition, MacCabe insists on the essential conservatism of such formal realisms. The texts of mass culture and high culture alike thus reveal a single underlying structure which functions to secure mass subservience to the dominant ideological discourse. Though MacCabe himself acquired a very public status during the Cambridge 'structuralist controversy', we should note that such anti-realist nostrums were in fact widely current at the time in radical intellectual circles.

Williams's own position, by contrast, represented what John Docker rightly terms a 'challenge to screen studies'. Docker cites *Television: Technology and Cultural Form*, referring to the ways in which Williams demonstrates, in defiance of *Screen* Theory, the clearly non-realist basis of much popular television (Docker, 1989:132–3). This is certainly so, though it is by no means Williams's express intention to argue thus against *Screen*. More to the point, it seems to me, though perhaps less to Docker's own liking, is Williams's much more sympathetic and much more historically nuanced account of literary and cultural realism itself. Williams was certainly no dogmatically Lukácsian socialist realist, but there was nonetheless an important sense in which his own literary sympathies, both practical and critical, were indeed of a distinctly realist kind. If the term has any literary-critical purchase at all, then the first two novels of Williams's Welsh trilogy (1960; 1964) are very clearly 'realist' in character; in *The Long Revolution*, he concluded the chapter on the contemporary novel with an insistence that 'a new realism is necessary, if we are to remain creative' (Williams, 1965:316); and his work on the drama had of course been preoccupied throughout with the 'naturalistic revolution'. In a lecture first delivered to a SEFT/ *Screen* weekend school in 1976, and shortly thereafter published in the journal itself, Williams mounted a spirited defence of realism, and did so moreover in ways which deliberately endorsed self-consciously radical, realist television, in this instance Allen, Garnett and Loach's *The Big Flame*. Though MacCabe is nowhere cited by name, the argument is very pointedly directed against analyses such as his. Realism, Williams argues, is much better understood in terms of intention, specifically the threefold intention to social extension, historical contemporaneity and secular action, than in terms of any particular formal method (Williams, 1989c:228–9). Furthermore, whenever we move to the level of specific analysis, Williams insists, both methods and intentions are highly variable (ibid.:239). The point, then, is not to reduce realism to a particular formal method, as MacCabe had done, but to pursue the 'analysis of a developing dramatic form and its variations' (ibid.).

Despite MacCabe's, and *Screen's*, repeated invocation of Brecht, it is clear in retrospect that it was Williams, the drama scholar, who was actually the much more properly Brechtian. For Brecht's central charge against Lukács had been that of the imposition of 'merely formal, literary criteria for realism' (Brecht, 1980:82), and this is exactly what MacCabe proposes, albeit negatively rather than positively valorised. Against Lukács (and others), Brecht had argued that 'They are . . . enemies of production. Production makes them uncomfortable . . . And they themselves don't want to produce' (Benjamin, 1973:118). Williams is surely right to detect an analogously formalist dogmatism at work in the newly emerging anti-realist orthodoxies. We live in a society, he writes,

> which is . . . rotten with criticism, in which the very frustrations of
> cultural production turn people from production to criticism . . .
> It is precisely because these makers [i.e. Allen, Garnett and Loach]
> are contemporaries engaged in active production, that we need
> not criticism but analysis . . . the complex seeing of analysis rather
> than . . . the abstractions of critical classification. (Williams,
> 1989c:239)

This seems to me very close to what should have been the last word on post-structuralist anti-realism.

It should not, of course, be read as the converse, a principled anti-modernism, such as Lukács had indeed engaged in, nor even a principled anti-postmodernism. Williams's later novels, we need note, are much more obviously 'experimental' in character than any simple notion of realism might lead one to expect. For Williams, there can be no general, formal characterisation either of 'modernism' or of 'realism', and the two cannot thereby be counterposed to each other as antithetical abstractions, in the manner envisaged by Lukács and, in effect, by MacCabe. Moreover, what matters most for a radical art is, for Williams, the capacity to point beyond the real: hence his sympathy for what he terms 'the alternative method of a hypothesis within . . . recognition', in *The Big Flame*, 'a hypothesis played out . . . within a politically imagined possibility' (Williams, 1989c:234). As Tony Pinkney has rather interestingly suggested, Williams might well have been not so much the 'British Lukács' as the British Ernst Bloch (Pinkney, 1989:28–31). This utopian impulse, most obviously present in *The Volunteers* (Williams, 1978b) and in *The Fight for Manod* (Williams, 1979c), connects, no doubt, to the stress on production, on what Williams was still willing to name 'creativity'. This is perhaps the most fundamental of differences between the various cultural materialisms deriving from Williams and the post-structuralisms deriving from *Screen*. The original, Althusserian, *Screen* position, which had lain stress on the ways in which the text positions the reader, was eventually to be superseded by a later, more properly deconstructionist sense of a multiplicity of possible readerly responses. Thus both Barker's *The Tremulous Private Body* (1984) and Belsey's *The Subject of Tragedy* (1985), for example, would each construct the literary-historical past as, to all intents and purposes, a narrative effect of the present. It is only in the cultural materialist line, from Williams, that such historiographical relativism is determinedly refused.

   The most significant figure in this latter line is almost certainly Terry Eagleton, professor of English at Oxford University. Though Eagleton clearly occupies a much less representative position in relation to literary studies than does, say, Stuart Hall in relation to cultural studies, the trajectory of his intellecual career nonetheless nicely traces the varying impact of Williams's work on radical literary criticism in Britain. Eagleton's early work (1968) is written very much in the shadow of *Culture and Society,* so much so, in fact, as apparently to excite some irritation even on Williams's part (Williams, 1979a:110). And as late as 1975, Eagleton's book-length study of the Brontës manages to combine a continuing debt to Williams with an emergent proto-Althusserianism (Eagleton, 1975). Only a year later, however, would come *Criticism and Ideology*, and with it not only a fairly full-blown Althusserianism, deriving in part from Pierre Macherey, but also a pointedly trenchant critique of Williams. The full-blown Althusserianism consists, on the one hand, in a highly formalist elaboration of 'the major constituents of a Marxist theory of literature', which centres around the twin concepts of 'mode of production' and 'ideology' (Eagleton, 1976:44–63); and on the other, in the proposal for a structuralist 'science of the text', which will take, as its theoretical object, the ways in which literature 'produces', in the sense of performs, ideology (ibid.:64–101).

The critique of Williams finds his work guilty, by turn, of an 'idealist epistemology, organicist aesthetics and corporatist sociology', all three of which have their roots in 'Romantic populism' (ibid.:27). The defining characteristic of that Romanticism, as of the very notion of 'culture' itself, is, for Eagleton, a radical 'over-subjectivising' of the social formation, in which structure is reduced to experience (ibid.:26). This is very much what Hall would later refer to as the 'experiential pull' in Williams and Thompson. But where Hall would, at least notionally, concede experience its due, Eagleton prosecutes a much more rigorously structuralist case. For Eagleton, meanings are not culture, but ideology; and it follows, then, that the new solidaristic values and meanings which, in Williams, are seen as the active creation of men and women in the historical present, can in fact only ever be '*enabled* by revolutionary rupture', at some point in the historical future (ibid.:27). Williams's 'generous reverence for human capacities' thus entails, in Eagleton's view, 'a drastic misconception of the structures of advanced capitalist formations' (ibid.:28). In short, Williams fails to understand the ways in which working–class subjectivity is determined by bourgeois ideology; 'structure of feeling' is thus an essentially inadequate conceptualisation of ideology, which misreads structure merely as pattern (ibid.:33–4); and even Williams's use of the Gramscian notion of hegemony is wrongly predicated on its experiential primacy and is, therefore, necessarily 'structurally undifferentiated' (ibid.:42). We can concede something to the power of Eagleton's critique of Williams's earlier culturalism, while insisting nonetheless on its markedly retrospective quality: Williams's later cultural materialism, which was already substantially formed by 1976, was to prove much less susceptible to such charges of empiricism. Moreover, in so far as real differences do indeed persist, it is surely Eagleton's position, rather than that of Williams, which is the more 'idealist and academicist' (ibid.:25). Eagleton's quintessentially Althusserian insistence on the determining power of ideology over the human subject is, as Thompson might say, '*exactly* what has commonly been designated, in the Marxist tradition, as idealism' (Thompson, 1978:205). It leads almost unavoidably to an enormous condescension toward popular activity, whether political or cultural. The equally Althusserian defence of the notion of aesthetic value, coupled as it was with both a substantive acceptance of the content of the literary canon and a passing sneer at the 'abstract egalitarianism' of cultural studies (ibid.:162–3), is similarly academicist. As Howard Felperin would unkindly observe: 'you can take the boy out of Cambridge, but you cannot take Cambridge out of the boy' (Felperin, 1985:57).

The intent of these remarks is not to take Eagleton to task for views he would in any case soon abandon but to emphasise the full extent to which structuralism and cultural materialism offered alternative, very different, and in some ways opposed, ways out of the theoretical deadlock between idealist humanism and determinist Marxism. These differences revolve around their respective concepts of structure, agency and subjectivity: for structuralism, structure was all-determining, agency an illusion and subjectivity the ideological effect of structure; for cultural materialism, structure sets limits and exerts pressures, agency takes place within those limits and pressures, and takes the characteristic form of an unavoidably material production, and subjectivity, though socially produced and shared, is nonetheless both real and active. The analytical logic of structuralism points towards a perennial search for the impress of ideology concealed within the deep structures of the text. Though the enabling rhetoric is both radical and contextual, the substantive focus remains the business as usual of literary-critical canonical exegesis. And though later post-structuralisms might dispute that focus, they certainly need not do so. Post-structuralism of the Derridean kind can very easily settle for little more than the substitution of a plurality of possible 'deconstructive' readings for the ideal of a singular, because scientific, 'structural' reading, while nonetheless preserving, and in a perverse way reinforcing, the canon of texts available for critical investigation. By contrast, the analytical logic of cultural materialism points towards a necessary decentring both of texts into the contexts of their production, reproduction and consumption, and of Literature into culture, literary studies into cultural studies. If Williams's politico-theoretical rhetoric was a great deal less 'revolutionary' than

Althusser's, the substantive case at issue is surely very much more so. Certainly, this was to prove Eagleton's own eventual assessment.

Eagleton's next two books, *Walter Benjamin* and *The Rape of Clarissa*, published in 1981 and 1982 respectively, represent that moment in his work in which a partial repudiation of Althusserianism coincides with both a horrified fascination for post-structuralism and a developing respect for cultural materialism. As we have already noted, this combination of repudiation, fascination and respect is actually announced in *Walter Benjamin*, a text whose major theoretical rationale remains, however, that of a political defence of a kind of revolutionary intransigence in an obviously non-revolutionary situation (Eagleton, 1985:139). The combination is much more properly constitutive of the argument in *The Rape of Clarissa*, where a kind of feminist deconstruction goes hand in hand with what Eagleton terms 'historical materialism', but which is surely, in its stress on 'literary modes of production' (Eagleton, 1982:viii), actually a cultural materialism. Following Habermas (1989), Eagleton proposes to understand this particular, eighteenth–century, mode of literary production as one formed within the context of the new bourgeois 'public sphere' (Eagleton, 1982:6–7). *The Rape of Clarissa* thus inaugurates an 'institutional' analysis of the social functions of literature and criticism, which will actually provide the central organising theme for what are Eagleton's most fully cultural materialist books to date, *Literary Theory* and *The Function of Criticism*. The first of these was, of course, a textbook, though the apparent conventionality of its form is belied by the subversive intent of its argument. Its critical and often hostile account of various contemporary schools of literary theory is predicated on an institutional history of the development of English studies as a discipline, and culminates in a polemical call for the kind of 'political criticism' that will go beyond the limits of the institution (Eagleton, 1983:17–53, 194–217). This argument is resumed and once again coupled to the Habermasian notion of the early bourgeois public sphere in *The Function of Criticism*, which was first published in 1984, though much of it had been written during Eagleton's 1983 visiting fellowship at the University of Melbourne. In both books the stress falls on the institutional production of criticism, as it had for Williams. In both, too, the category of 'Literature' is radically decentred (Eagleton,

1983:16, 197; 1984:107–8), as it had also been for Williams. In the later book, moreover, Eagleton specifically invokes Williams as 'the most important critic of post-war Britain', whose concept of 'structure of feeling' he deems 'vital' in 'examining the *articulations* between different sign-systems and practices' (Eagleton, 1984:108–10). Generous though this may be, the compliment is actually less telling than the more general cultural materialism of the argument in which it occurs.

Eagleton's most recent work, *The Ideology of the Aesthetic*, is a powerfully persuasive critical history of the concept of the aesthetic, as it has evolved in modern, (mainly) German thought, from Baumgarten to Habermas. Much less concerned with institutional analysis, the book has in fact been criticised as inclined both to 'over-value theory' and to ignore the social organisation of aesthetics (During, 1991:177, 180–1). Eagleton actually concedes the latter point, or very nearly so, in his own Introduction, but stresses that one simply cannot write about everything (Eagleton, 1990:5). And in truth sometimes theory does have to be taken seriously as theory. For the central purpose of Eagleton's argument here, in contradistinction, say, to the Griffith school's radically relativist sociologising, is to recover both the negative and the positive moments within the 'aesthetic' tradition. The obvious, but little remarked upon, point of comparison is with Williams's own account of the English 'culturalist' tradition in *Culture and Society*: as Eagleton notes, 'the Anglophone tradition is in fact derivative of German philosophy' (ibid.:11). Just as, in the prosperously utilitarian 1950s, it took a Welshman to seek out the positively emancipatory content of the derivative English tradition itself, so in the darkly utilitarian 1980s, a Lancashire Irishman has discovered something at least of the same in the German original. Indeed, the book might well have been titled *Kultur und Gesellschaft 1750–1980*, though, alas, that is not the form of the actually existing German translation of *Culture and Society* (Williams, 1972). The point of all this is not to celebrate Eagleton's recantation from an earlier Althusserian apostasy, nor his return to the fold of Anglo-culturalist empiricism. For in truth there can be no apostasy where there is no orthodoxy, and Williams's cultural materialism was not so much a doctrine as a research project. Nor, despite erstwhile Anglo-Althusserian charges to the contrary, was Williams really in any fold, of either English or empiricist extraction. The point, then, is simply to suggest the uses to which Williams's cultural materialism can be put in hands as creative as Eagleton's. The latter's own judgement warrants repetition: 'the notion of cultural materialism is . . . of considerable value . . . It extends and completes Marx's own struggle against idealism, carrying it forcefully into that realm ("culture") always most ideologically resistant to materialist redefinition' (Eagleton, 1989a:169). Though Eagleton still insists on the base/ superstructure formula and on the general priority of historical materialism, he nonetheless concedes that a 'cultural materialist concern for . . . social and material conditions . . . carried into the academic institutions, would make the most profound difference to what actually got done there' (ibid.). For a professor of English, for the meantime at any rate, this might well be quite a lot to be going on with.

5

Post-Culturalism and the Politics of Theory

Thus far we have discussed Williams's work, and cultural materialism more generally, mainly in relation to the specifics of British and Australian intellectual life. But neither the history of British cultural studies nor that of the wider postwar Anglophone intellectual culture can be written in such circumscribed terms: in so far as the intelligentsia is concerned, perhaps the single most important development over the last thirty years has been the relatively rapid rate of translation of key theoretical texts between the major western European languages, in particular English, French and German. The impress of French structuralism and German critical theory remains continuously present in the British, American and Australian debates. More importantly, perhaps, we need to note the presence of roughly commensurate sets of theoretical dilemmas in other intellectual cultures powerfully subject to the simultaneous influence of literary humanism and Communist Marxism. The obviously relevant instances here are France and Germany, the two European countries which provided a home to Western Marxism, and to date the only western countries to witness the creation and subsequent destruction of mass Communist Parties. In this chapter, then, we proceed to a brief comparison between British cultural materialism and certain roughly equivalent developments in recent French and German thought: Foucault's 'genealogy', Bourdieu's cultural sociology, and Habermas's theory of communicative action.

We have had cause already to compare cultural materialism with various forms of structuralism and post-structuralism. It might be imagined, then, that there is little more to be said about Foucault certainly, perhaps even about Bourdieu. It might also be argued that, in the strictest sense of the term, neither Foucault nor Bourdieu can be considered properly 'post-structuralist'; that the title belongs much more appropriately to Derrida's deconstructive criticism, as also to that of the later Barthes. Unlike Barthes, Foucault himself deliberately refused the self-description 'structuralist' (Foucault, 1980:114); and moreover, as structuralism gave way to post-structuralism, he was to prove publicly dismissive of Derridean deconstruction (Foucault, 1972a:602). Somewhat analogously, Bourdieu sought to distance himself from the 'objectivism' of structuralist anthropology (Bourdieu, 1977a:1–30); and he too was to prove similarly dismissive of Derrida (Bourdieu, 1984:495). And yet there is a sense in which both inhabit a more generally post- structuralist intellectual universe. As noted in chapter four, from Durkheim's structural anthropology and Saussure's early structural linguistics through to the later 'high structuralism' of Barthes and Lévi-Strauss, French structuralism displayed an aspiration to scientificity, its central project to discover the truth beneath the text hidden within the text's own deep structures. By contrast, post-structuralism has betrayed that aspiration by an insistence that there is no such single truth in the text, that cultural meaning can never be pinned down. And this scepticism *vis-à-vis* discourse, a scepticism which seeks to identify the possibilities within discourse which discourse itself seeks to repress, is in fact as characteristic of Foucault and Bourdieu as of Derrida and Barthes.

More importantly for our purposes, both Foucault and Bourdieu take much more seriously than does its author Derrida's insistence that deconstruction, as distinct from critique, should interfere 'with solid structures, "material" institutions, and not only with discourses or signifying representations' (Derrida, 1987:19). For Foucault, institutional and discursive practices, powers and knowledges, are inextricably interconnected, and in ways that are necessarily internal to each other. Thus, when he rejects the Marxist base/superstructure model, Foucault does so in terms oddly reminiscent of Williams, which stress not simply the autonomy of the 'superstructures', but more importantly their materiality (Foucault, 1980:118). For Bourdieu, too, the 'symbolic power' of ideology is not some secondary effect of an economy located elsewhere, but is itself fully material. Thus when Bourdieu rejects the 'crude reductionism' of much Marxism, he does so, again in terms oddly reminiscent of Williams, by emphasising that ideologies 'owe their structure and their most specific functions to the social conditions of their production and circulation—that is to say, to the functions which they fulfil . . . for the specialists competing for the monopoly of the established competence in question' (Bourdieu, 1977b:116). If cultural materialism reduced to essentials holds simply, in Bennett's phrase, 'that cultural practices should be regarded as forms of material production' (Bennett, 1990:13), then clearly there is much, both in Foucault and perhaps even more so in Bourdieu, that is in this generic sense 'cultural materialist'.

There are nonetheless very significant differences between Williams's cultural materialism and that of both Foucault and Bourdieu. The contrast with Foucault is particularly striking. Where Williams persists in seeing a history and an evolution, a long revolution that is in some quite fundamental senses progressive, Foucault detects only difference and rupture. *Discipline and Punish*, as much as the earlier, more fully structuralist, *Madness and Civilisation* and *The Birth of the Clinic*, are each built around binary oppositions between the classical *episteme* of the eighteenth century, on the one hand, and our own modern *episteme*, on the other. These discursive regimes are contrasted with each other as equally systemic, equally valid, equally regulative. There is, then, no progress, only difference, and at times Foucault's remorseless demystification of the pretensions to scientificity of modern psychiatry, medicine and penology appears almost to suggest a preference for eighteenth–century 'authenticity'. Where Williams persists in seeing the possibilities for a macropolitics that will continue the long revolution, and for a kind of intellectual engagement that will be at worst 'organic' to the working class, at best 'universal', Foucault aspires, as we have seen, only to a 'specific' micropolitics. Where Williams persists in seeing human society and culture as the products of human agency, albeit an agency that is often alienated from itself, Foucault's position remains resolutely anti-humanist. The strength of the new sciences of psychoanalysis and structural anthropology, he writes in 1966, is in their ability 'to do without the concept of man . . . they dissolve man' (Foucault, 1973b:379). This anti-humanism clearly persists from the earlier archaeology into the middle–period genealogy: 'genealogy', he insists, requires 'a form of history which can account for the constitution of knowledges . . . without having to make reference to a subject' (Foucault, 1980:117).

Foucault's historical relativism and his modestly libertarian micropolitics remain connected to this anti-humanism by way not so much of a presence as of an absence: that of an ethics. Where Williams's humanist historiography and humanist epistemology both sustain and are sustained by a humanist ethic, there is no such equivalent in Foucault. This is not to suggest that a practical ethics is necessarily logically incompatible with a theoretical anti-humanism, only that Foucault himself is unable to construct one until the later volumes of *The History of Sexuality*, and that when it does appear it is a poor, pathetic thing, an aestheticist mythologisation of the phallocratic sexual mores of a bunch of Greek slave–owners (Foucault, 1985). Williams's humanism is not, of course, the 'liberal humanism' so often derided, and rightly so, by both Althusserian Marxists and post-structuralist feminists for its false universalism. It is, rather, a specifically 'materialist' humanism, which acknowledges the differences in our present condition, precisely so as to distinguish eradicable inequity from desirable plurality, and thereby to proceed not to the abstractly universal but to a concrete commonality. In a world which becomes progressively more totalised, by the pressure of global environmental crisis as much as by the drive toward a 'New World Order', Foucault's refusal of a humanist ethics, as also that in post-structuralism generally, seems closer to an ethic of irresponsibility than to one of self-mastery.

Bourdieu's work is much closer to Williams in tone, purpose and subject matter, and clearly excited the latter's positive admiration. In his 1988 obituary, Garnham makes something of a virtue out of the necessity that Williams 'was a man who worked, largely alone with the assistance of his wife, outside the institutional bases of communication studies . . . He never received foundation or research council funding for communications research' (Garnham, 1988:124). That this might have been at best a cruel virtue is suggested by the results of such relatively well funded, collaborative research as has been undertaken by Bourdieu. The obvious instance here is *Distinction*, an immensely sophisticated piece of work, both in theory and in method, which is built around an extremely detailed sociological survey, by interview and by ethnographic observation, of the cultural preferences of over twelve hundred people in Paris, Lille and a small French provincial town (Bourdieu, 1984:503). The points of similarity between Bourdieu and Williams are at some levels readily apparent: a shared sense of the continuing importance of social class to the social structures of advanced capitalism; a shared suspicion of the pretensions to exclusive legitimacy of bourgeois 'high culture'; a shared sympathy for popular cultural aspirations; and a shared assessment of the centrality of culture to the social organisation of contemporary capitalism. Bourdieu's pointed contrast between 'the aesthetic disposition' of legitimate taste, on the one hand, which 'presupposes the distance from the world . . . which is the basis of bourgeois experience' (ibid.:54), and 'the popular aesthetic', on the other, 'based on the affirmation of continuity between art and life' and 'a deep-rooted demand for participation' (ibid.:32), both echoes and confirms much of what Williams had argued about modernism, postmodernism and popular culture. At a further, perhaps deeper level, there is an interesting parallelism between Williams's theory of determination and Bourdieu's theory of practice. Both attempt to theorise human sociality in terms of the strategic action of individuals within a constraining, but nonetheless not determining, context of values, a 'structure of feeling' in Williams, the 'habitus' in Bourdieu (Bourdieu, 1977a:72–95). These are understood, in each case, as simultaneously structured and structuring, as materially produced (ibid.:72), and, interestingly, as very often generation-specific (ibid.:78).

But there are important differences too. Where Williams insists on the concretely experiential quality of such structures, the equivalent in Bourdieu is much more abstract, a system of durable dispositions rather than a pattern of felt experience. Where Williams works with a model of theory as explicitly critical, Bourdieu affects a quasi-positivistic objectivism. Though *Distinction* is indeed 'a social critique of the judgement of taste', it is much less obviously a critique of the aesthetic disposition itself: here the moment of critique remains well concealed behind a carefully cultivated mask of scientific 'objectivity'. Where Williams conceives of the intellectual function as critical, and of intellectuals as significantly productive of emergent sensibility, Bourdieu detects mainly the dominated fraction of the dominant class, the self-interested traders in cultural capital. There is thus a certain cynical quality to Bourdieu's insistence that 'all practices, including those purporting to be disinterested or gratuitous' can be treated as 'economic practices directed towards the maximizing of material or symbolic profit' (ibid.:183). That cynicism leads easily to a radical overestimation of the reproductive powers of the social status quo—hence what Garnham and Williams (1986:129) term the 'functionalist/determinist residue' in Bourdieu's concept of reproduction, a residue that might well prove much more than residual. Though Garnham and Williams resist the description, it does seem to me that Bourdieu's work is best understood in its relation to Durkheimian structural anthropology: the positivistic rendering of the empirical as the externally measurable and observable, the sense of the efficacy of collective representations, even the conception of 'sociology' as embracing what the English speakers still distinguish as 'anthropology', all this is characteristically Durkheimian. Indeed, one might venture the suggestion that Bourdieu stands in much the same relation to French anthropology—dissenting, plebeian, but belonging, nonetheless—as had the young Williams to English Literature. It matters, then, and more than Garnham and Williams acknowledge, that, in so far as they are visible at all, Bourdieu's politics appear essentially relativistic. In Bourdieu, as in Foucault, the structuralist legacy leads to a systematic derogation of the possibilities for progressive social change, collective action and individual politico-ethical commitment. In both it is the initial, structuralist insistence on theoretical anti-humanism, rather than any particular, consequent theoretical or analytical strategy, which proves fundamentally disabling. Durkheim and Saussure have a lot to answer for.

Habermas's work, too, can be represented as, in a significant sense, cultural materialist. More sympathetic to Marx than either Foucault or Bourdieu, Habermas interprets the base/superstructure model, very much as Williams does, as a historical rather than ontological proposition, 'the mark of a seal that must be broken' (Habermas, 1990:16). His early theorisation of the bourgeois 'public sphere' (Habermas, 1989), as also the later borrowing from Max Weber of the notion of increasingly autonomous and professionalised cultural spheres as constitutive of a distinctive cultural modernity (Habermas, 1985:9), both suggest the possibilities for an institutional analysis of culture. Habermas's theoretical affiliations have been to Western Marxism, of course, rather than to structuralism: 'I value being considered a Marxist', he declared, at a time when such assertions had long since ceased to be fashionable in the western European intelligentsia (Habermas, 1979a:33). More specifically, Habermas has affirmed his own indebtedness to 'Lukács, Korsch, Gramsci and the Frankfurt School' (Habermas, 1979b:83), that is, to the more expressly humanist and culturalist elements within the Western Marxist legacy. This is a Marxism which learnt much from Weber and from German sociology, most importantly that modern capitalism remains subject to a developmental logic of rationalisation. Weber's rationalisation thesis, as also his elaboration of the different types of rational action, are central to Habermas. Indeed, the latter's defence of Enlightenment reason, against both French post-structuralism and the darkly pessimistic 'dialectic of Enlightenment' of his own former mentors Adorno and Horkheimer (Habermas, 1987a), can be seen as resuming the earlier meliorist expectations not only of Marx but of Weber. There are obvious parallels between Williams and Habermas, and these have on occasion been remarked upon (Eagleton, 1990:404, 409; Koh, 1991). Both subscribe to a kind of radical-democratic anti-capitalism which takes its inspiration partly from Marxism, partly from post-Romantic idealism, in Habermas's case that of Weber, in Williams's that of Leavis. Both are as enthusiastically sympathetic to the postmodern 'new social move ments' (Habermas, 1981) as they are suspicious of postmodern theoretical relativism. For Habermas, as for Williams, the long revolution continues, but it does so in the peculiar guise of a reason immanent within sociality itself. For Habermas, as for Williams, the theoretical model of an emancipated culture, deriving from the allegedly constitutive properties of actually existing culture, provides the criteria by which both to critique existing social reality and to elaborate the utopian possibilities for real social change. For Williams the model is that of a truly 'common culture', for Habermas that of unimpeded communication: through the structure of language, he writes, 'autonomy and responsibility are posited for us. Our first sentence expresses unequivocally the intention of universal and unconstrained consensus' (Habermas, 1971:314). The end result is the theory of communicative action itself (Habermas, 1984; 1987a).

Habermas's departures from Communist Marxism are at least as radical as those of Williams, and in one respect very much more so: for Habermas, the old class struggle between capital and labour has been rendered archaic by the emergence of the postwar welfare state on the one hand, the struggles of the new social movements on the other (Habermas, 1981:33). As empirical propositions about the nature of contemporary social reality, these seem to me highly implausible, even when applied to the unusually affluent working class and unusually influential Green movement of the Federal German Republic. Williams's sense of the continuing importance of social class seems to me much more persuasive. Quite apart from this fundamental political difference, there are differences also of intellectual approach, which are partly disciplinary and partly national-cultural in origin. For Williams, the concretely experiential remains stubbornly relevant, not so much as the antithesis but as the complement to abstract reason. As Eagleton rightly observes: 'Williams's subtle sense of the complex mediations between such necessarily universal formations as social class, and the lived particularities of place, region, Nature, the body, contrasts tellingly with Habermas's universalist rationalism' (Eagleton, 1990:409). It is my guess that, for Williams, class was as much a matter of lived particularity as of universal formation, and that it was at this level, as much as at any other, that he chose to refuse the false opposition between old and new social movements. Be that as it may, it seems difficult to avoid the conclusion that for Habermas, as for Bourdieu, the disciplinary claims of sociology/anthropology appear to pose a recurrent threat to the claims of particularity. That this is as much the case in the German humanistic tradition as in the French structuralist serves to remind us of the ways in which both cultural studies and Williams's cultural materialism emerged from a distinctively British intellectual environment barely touched by sociology. This may not be quite the burden that it once seemed.

Although Williams and Habermas, Foucault and Bourdieu do indeed, as we have seen, have a certain 'cultural materialism' in common, significant divergences nonetheless also arise between their respective positions, and these are at least in part explicable as a consequence of 'inherited' differences between British culturalism, French structuralism and German critical theory. In short, Williams stands in an essentially analogous relation to the culturalist tradition as do Foucault and Bourdieu to the structuralist, Habermas to the (Western) Marxist: his cultural materialism is not so much culturalist, nor even left-culturalist, as positively *post-culturalist*. As we saw in chapter two, the theoretical literature in cultural studies has often contrasted Williams's 'culturalism' with the long tradition of French 'structuralism'. Post-structuralism developed as a reaction precisely against this structuralist intellectual tradition. But, as we also observed in chapter two, there is in fact an equivalently long culturalist intellectual tradition behind Williams, reaching back from Eliot and Leavis to Arnold and beyond. And Williams stands in relation to this tradition very much as what I have termed a 'post-culturalist'. This is so in more than the simply chronological sense. In its discovery that all knowledge is social and all meaning plural, post-structuralism discovered the futility of the structuralist aspiration to scientificity. Practically, this led to an emergent preoccupation with reader response, reception, the role of the reader, and similar related concepts. Before Williams, the culturalist tradition had typically subscribed, not to a scientism certainly, but nonetheless to a kind of 'objective idealism' by which truth was seen to inhere in the cultural tradition itself. Williams's own deconstruction of this notion, through the idea of the selective tradition, effects a relativising turn similar to that of post-structuralism in relation to structuralism. It does so by virtue of an appeal to the role of the (collective) reader. It more than gestures in the direction of a recognition of the intrication of power within discourse such as is acknowledged by both Foucault and Bourdieu; and a recognition of the materiality, historicity and social arbitrariness of the linguistic sign similar to that in Foucault and Derrida. And all of this remains coupled to a sense of genuinely free communicative action—a truly common culture—as normative, of which even Habermas might have approved. Little wonder, then, that Eagleton would eventually conclude that 'Williams's work has prefigured and pre-empted the development of parallel left positions by, so to speak, apparently standing still' (Eagleton, 1984:109).

Practically consequent though they may be, the differences between Williams and Habermas are theoretically much less substantial and much less fundamental than those between Williams and French post-structuralism. Given sufficient evidence, life after death and a suitably tolerant heavenly discursive regimen, it will one day be possible for either Habermas or Williams to win round the other, without any significant concession over issues of principle. Things are rather different, however, in the particular corner of purgatory reserved for the care of the disembodied, decentred self. Theoretically, the central point at issue between cultural materialism and post-structuralism concerns neither the autonomy nor the effectivity nor even the materiality of culture, but rather the ontological status of the human subject, that is, the question of theoretical humanism versus theoretical anti-humanism. I am myself reasonably convinced that Williams, and Marx, though not most Marxists, are right in this matter: that there is, in fact, a human nature, and that this nature is best grasped by Marx's understanding of the human 'species being' as constituted by our capacity for conscious, collective and creative production (Marx, 1975:327–30). We are, then, quite centrally the makers of our own history and the producers of our own culture. It is because Williams holds to this view that his cultural materialism becomes, at its core, a theory of cultural *production*. And it is in this sense that it is indeed, as he insisted, 'a Marxist theory'. Such propositions are necessarily pregnant with political consequence. For these respective humanisms and anti-humanisms bear very differently not only on literary and cultural studies, considered as specialist academic disciplines, but also on the wider prospects for an emancipatory politics.

In the Foreword to their *Political Shakespeare*, Jonathan Dollimore and Alan Sinfield describe cultural materialism as an approach which combines 'historical context, theoretical method, political commitment and textual analysis' (Dollimore and Sinfield, 1985:vii). The political commitment here is of a necessarily radical kind, moreover: 'socialist and feminist commitment', they continue, 'confronts the conservative categories in which most criticism has . . . been conducted' (ibid.). There can be no doubt that Williams's own work was so politically motivated, nor that his was a deliberately radical politics. The possibility remains, however, that this is a matter of mere contingency. The nexus between political and cultural theory certainly seems so in the structuralist tradition, for example: the major French structuralist and post-structuralist thinkers have proved able to shift their political opinions, very often from left to right, without any corresponding amendment to their respective theoretical positions. But in Williams's cultural materialism, a simultaneous stress on the human capacity for conscious creativity on the one hand, on the material determination of the possibilities and limits of such creativity on the other, does seem very much more amenable to alignment with an emancipatory than with an exploitative or oppressive politics.

For Williams himself this meant a continuing commitment to the radical libertarian and socialist currents within the labour movement, and later a developing sympathy for Welsh nationalism. In both cases, the more obviously communitarian and solidaristic aspects of the politics sit fairly comfortably with equivalently communitarian and solidaristic elements in the cultural theory. As Williams told a 1977 Summer School of the Welsh nationalist party, Plaid Cymru, a 'truly prospective', as distinct from 'merely retrospective', radical nationalist politics could produce 'the kind of complex liberation which genuine community . . . could be' (Williams, 1989b:117–18).

Williams knew, of course, that Labour governments have been as much a part of the problem as of the solution; he knew too that the building of nation–states had been 'intrinsically a ruling-class operation' (Williams, 1983:181); he even knew that Welsh nationalism in the 1930s had been 'on the cultural Right . . . Wales was offered . . . as the last noble fragment of a classical and catholic world' (Williams, 1989c:59). His own socialism, as also his own Welshness, were of a very different kind. But the objection remains that even such labourisms and such radical nationalisms as his, whatever their original emancipatory intent, articulate a by now demonstrably residual, rather than emergent, structure of feeling, in a world that is increasingly internationalised, increasingly post-industrial, increasingly individualised, in short, increasingly 'postmodern'. Hence O'Connor and Redhead's damning comment 'that we are not going to hear', from Williams, 'anything that may shock the sensibilities of the "Labour Movement"' (O'Connor and Redhead, 1991:125). Such charges are particularly telling when made from the vantage point of a postmodern feminism, since the old working class or old Welsh community, as much as Habermas's 'life world', was sustained, both in reality and very often also as a normative ideal, by a sexual division of labour that was obviously patriarchal. It is not that feminists have ignored Williams (cf. Mitchell, 1966; Rowbotham, 1985; Lovell, 1989), nor even that Williams had entirely ignored feminism: when challenged in 1979, he readily conceded that it was not only a political weakness but 'an intellectual failing not to confront the problem' (Williams, 1979a:150). Both in the *Politics and Letters* interviews and in the later *Towards 2000*, there is evidence of a real attempt at solidarity with the new women's movement, for example, in his support for 'the transitional demand of payment for housework' (ibid.:149). But it is clear that Williams himself is never able adequately either to theorise or even to articulate emotionally such questions of sexual politics. As Bronwen Levy concludes, Williams offers little help 'in writing the particularities of the problems the family—or other social institutions—pose for many women'; and yet, she continues, 'in his insistence . . . on speaking his own class position, his ability to create disciplines and literary forms that enable that position to be spoken . . . he offers an important example' (Levy, 1989:110). One might go further and argue, with Carol Watts, that, whatever the limitations of Williams's own particular effort, cultural materialism itself can 'contribute to a feminist historical materialism' and 'connect[s] with a field of feminist study which is thriving— women's culture and literature, theories of representation' (Watts, 1989:106).

Whatever Williams's weaknesses as a feminist, O'Connor and Redhead's comments seem to me both manifestly false and manifestly unfair. On the contrary, Williams's later work engages very directly with the postmodern politics of the 1980s. It was in *Towards 2000* that Williams most clearly registered the paradigm shift from, as it were, the 'New New Left' to the 'postmodern left' that had occurred between the 1970s and the 1980s. While there are certain obvious continuities, for example between the ecological arguments advanced here and older themes aired in *The Country and the City*, *Towards 2000* is nonetheless characterised by a sustained attempt at theoretical innovation and exploration. Its most explicitly 'postmodern' moment, and one which entails a radical reversal of sensibilities within Williams's writing, is in its strong sense of the internationalisation of the contemporary world order. This provides the materials for a critique both of 'official' nationalism and of Labour's complicity therewith. To the 'official community' of nation–states such as 'the Yookay', Williams seeks to counterpose an internationalism that is nonetheless compatible with the 'lived and formed identities' of the 'minority peoples', not only the Welsh, but the Scots, Irish and West Indian, and even the English 'regions' (Williams, 1983:197). If this concern with localised, 'knowable' communities is not in itself novel, the radical antipathy to the British nation–state and to its culture most certainly is: the particularities of the Welsh and the complexities of a 'paranational' world system both become more pressing than the peculiarities of a Britain understood as English, an England understood as 'the South', a South understood as its ruling and intermediate classes. Moreover, Williams also quite deliberately identifies the new social movements—the peace movement, the ecology movement, the feminist movement, and the movement of 'oppositional culture'—as major 'resources for a journey of hope' beyond capitalism (ibid.:249–50). One clear measure of the distance travelled by Williams since the 1970s is provided by his ability here to recognise and applaud the achievements both of feminist scholarship and of the women's movement itself (ibid.:249).

Despite O'Connor and Redhead, the labour parties do not, in fact, figure as such a resource in *Towards 2000*, but rather as a problem to be negotiated. The central function of these parties, Williams writes, 'is to reproduce the existing definitions of issues and interests. When they extend to new issues and interests, they usually lead them back into a system which will isolate, dilute and eventually compromise them' (ibid.:250). This is a proposition which surely would offend the sensibilities of much of the labour movement, both in Britain and in Australia. Lesley Johnson even reads Williams's argument as tantamount to the suggestion that the new social movements now effectively challenge the very basis of the traditional institutions of the labour movement (Johnson, 1987:175). And in one sense this is so, for Williams is indisputably arguing against the labour parties as they have traditionally functioned. Johnson nonetheless underestimates the strength of Williams's commitment to class politics as such. For Williams, it is a *misinterpretation* to see social movements as 'getting beyond class politics' (ibid.:172). These new issues, followed through, in Williams's view, 'lead us into the central systems of the industrial-capitalist mode of production and . . . into its system of classes' (ibid.:172–3). For the Williams of *Towards 2000*, it is true, the labour movement can 'go either way'. But this is an alternative in which only one option is truly bearable: for if labour becomes finally incorporated, then socialism will be 'left stranded as a theory and a sect' (ibid.:173). What is true is that Williams, unlike Thompson, had by now clearly understood the labour parties, if not the labour movement, and certainly not the working class, as obstacles to social change. If O'Connor and Redhead require of a radical politics that it positively disengage not only from Labourism as a political ideology and a party but from the very notion of class itself, then they ask much more than that Williams should shock the sensibilities of the labour movement. They ask, in short, that he abandon the central insights not only of Marxism but of much mainstream academic sociology into the operation of structured social inequality within advanced capitalism. It hardly seems a price worth paying. It is, in my view, precisely in the strength both of Williams's endorsement of the new social movements, and of his deliberately nuanced appraisal of the labour movement, that he succeeds in recuperating the positive, but not the negative and fashionably *déclassé*, moment within postmodern leftism: 'The real struggle has broadened so much', Williams wrote in *Towards 2000*, 'the decisive issues have so radically changed, that only a new kind of socialist movement, fully contemporary in its ideas and methods, bringing a wide range of needs and interests together in a new definition of the general interest, has any real future' (ibid.:174). This seems to me about as right as we are likely to get it.

Bibliography

Adorno, T. and M. Horkheimer, (1972) *Dialectic of Enlightenment*, trans. J. Cumming, New York: Herder & Herder
—— (1979) *Dialectic of Enlightenment*, trans. J. Cumming, London: Verso
Althusser, L. (1969) *For Marx*, trans. B. Brewster, London: Allen Lane
—— (1971) *Lenin and Philosophy and Other Essays*, trans. B. Brewster, London: New Left Books
Althusser, L. and É. Balibar (1970) *Reading Capital*, trans. B. Brewster, London: New Left Books
Anderson, P. (1970) 'Components of the National Culture' in A. Cockburn and R. Blackburn (eds) *Student Power*, Harmondsworth: Penguin
—— (1976) *Considerations on Western Marxism*, London: New Left Books
—— (1980) *Arguments Within English Marxism*, London: New Left Books
Baldick, C. (1983) *The Social Mission of English Criticism 1848-1932*, Oxford: Oxford University Press
Barker, F. (1984) *The Tremulous Private Body: Essays on Subjection*, London: Methuen
Barthes, R. (1968) *Elements of Semiology*, trans. A. Levers and C. Smith, New York: Hill & Wang
—— (1974) *S/Z*, trans. R. Miller, New York: Hill & Wang

—— (1975) *The Pleasure of the Text*, trans. R. Miller, New York: Hill & Wang

—— (1976) *Sade, Fourier, Loyola*, trans. R. Miller, Hill & Wang

—— (1977) *Image–Music–Text*, trans. S. Heath, New York: Hill & Wang

Belsey, C. (1980) *Critical Practice*, London: Methuen

—— (1985) *The Subject of Tragedy: Identity and Difference in Renaissance Drama*, London: Methuen

Benjamin, W. (1973) *Understanding Brecht*, trans. A. Bostock, London: New Left Books

Bennett, T. (1979) *Formalism and Marxism*, London: Methuen

—— (1985) 'Really Useless "Knowledge": A Political Critique of Aesthetics' *Thesis Eleven*, 12

—— (l986) 'Introduction: Popular Culture and "The Turn to Gramsci"' in T. Bennett et al. (eds) *Popular Culture and Social Relations*, Milton Keynes: Open University Press

—— (1989) 'Holding Spaces' *Southern Review*, 22, 2

—— (1990) *Outside Literature*, London: Routledge

Bennett, T. et al. (eds) (1981) *Culture, Ideology and Social Process: A Reader*, London: Batsford Academic/Open University Press

—— (eds) (1986) *Popular Culture and Social Relations*, Milton Keynes: Open University Press

Bentham, J. (1962) 'The Rationale of Reward' in *The Works of Jeremy Bentham*, Vol.2, New York: Russell & Russell

Bourdieu, P. (1977a) *Outline of a Theory of Practice*, trans. R. Nice, Cambridge: Cambridge University Press

—— (1977b) 'Symbolic Power', trans. C. Wringe, in D. Gleeson (ed.) *Identity and Structure: Issues in the Sociology of Education*, Driffield: Nafferton Books

—— (1984) *Distinction: A Social Critique of the Judgement of Taste*, trans. R. Nice, London: Routledge & Kegan Paul

Brecht, B. (1980) 'Against Georg Lukács', trans. S. Hood, in E. Bloch et al. *Aesthetics and Politics*, London: Verso

Bukharin, N. (1977) 'Poetry, Poetics and the Problems of Poetry in the U.S.S.R.' in M. Gorky et al. *Soviet Writers' Congress 1934: The Debate on Socialist Realism and Modernism*, London: Lawrence and Wishart

Caudwell, C. (1946) *Illusion and Reality*, London: Lawrence and Wishart

Centre for Contemporary Cultural Studies (1978) *On Ideology*, London: Hutchinson/Centre for Contemporary Cultural Studies

Clarke, J. et al. (1976) 'Subcultures, Cultures and Class: A Theoretical Overview' in S. Hall and T. Jefferson (eds) *Resistance Through Rituals: Youth Sub-cultures in Post-war Britain*, London: Hutchinson/Centre for Contemporary Cultural Studies

—— (eds) (1979) *Working-Class Culture: Studies in History and Theory*, London: Hutchinson/Centre for Contemporary Cultural Studies

Coleridge, S. T. (1972) *On the Constitution of the Church and State*, London: J. M. Dent

Collins, R. et al. (eds) (1986a) *Media, Culture and Society: A Critical Reader*, London: Sage

—— (1986b) Introduction in R. Collins et al. (eds) *Media, Culture and Society: A Critical Reader*, London: Sage

—— (1988) *The Economics of Television: The U.K. Case*, London: Sage

Curran, J. (1979) 'The Media and Politics' *Media, Culture and Society* 1, 1

Curran, J. and J. Seaton, (1981) *Power Without Responsibility: The Press and Broadcasting in Britain*, Glasgow: Fontana

Curran, J. et al. (eds) (1977) *Mass Communication and Society*, London: Edward Arnold

Dermody, S. et al. (1982) 'Introduction: Australian Cultural Studies: Problems and Dilemmas' in S. Dermody et al. (eds) *Nellie Melba, Ginger Meggs and Friends: Essays in Australian Cultural History*, Malmsbury: Kibble Books

Derrida, J. (1973) *Speech and Phenomena and Other Essays on Husserl's Theory of Signs*, trans. D. B. Allison, Evanston: Northwestern University Press

—— (1974) *Of Grammatology*, trans. G. C. Spivak, Baltimore: Johns Hopkins University Press

—— (1978) *Writing and Difference*, trans. A. Bass, Chicago: University of Chicago Press

—— (1982) *Margins of Philosophy*, trans. A. Bass, Chicago: University of Chicago Press

—— (1987) *The Truth in Painting*, trans. G. Bennington and I. McLeod, Chicago: University of Chicago Press

Docker, J. (1989) 'Williams' Challenge to Screen Studies' *Southern Review* 22, 2

Dollimore, J. (1985) 'Introduction: Shakespeare, Cultural Materialism and the New Historicism' in J. Dollimore and A. Sinfield (eds) *Political Shakespeare: New Essays in Cultural Materialism*, Manchester: Manchester University Press

Dollimore, J. and A. Sinfield (1985) 'Foreword: Cultural Materialism' in J. Dollimore and A. Sinfield (eds) *Political Shakespeare: New Essays in Cultural Materialism*, Manchester: Manchester University Press

Doyle, B. (1982) 'The Hidden History of English Studies' in P. Widdowson (ed.) *Re-Reading English*, London: Methuen

During, S. (1991) 'The Ideology of the Aesthetic' *Arena* 94

Durkheim, E. (1964) *The Division of Labor in Society*, trans. G. Simpson, New York: Free Press

—— (1976) *The Elementary Forms of the Religious Life*, trans. J. W. Swain, London: George Allen & Unwin

Eagleton, T. (1968) 'The Idea of a Common Culture' in T. Eagleton and B. Wicker (eds) *From Culture to Revolution: The Slant Symposium 1967*, London: Sheed & Ward

—— (1975) *Myths of Power: A Marxist Study of the Brontës*, London: Macmillam

—— (1976) *Criticism and Ideology*, London: New Left Books

—— (1981) *Walter Benjamin or Towards a Revolutionary Criticism*, London: Verso

—— (1982) *The Rape of Clarissa: Writing, Sexuality and Class Struggle in Samuel Richardson*, Oxford: Basil Blackwell

—— (1983) *Literary Theory: An Introduction*, Oxford: Basil Blackwell

—— (1984) *The Function of Criticism: From 'The Spectator' to Post-Structuralism*, London: Verso

—— (1985) 'Criticism and Ideology: Andrew Milner Interviews Terry Eagleton' *Thesis Eleven* 12

—— (1986) *Against the Grain: Essays 1975-1985*, London: Verso

—— (1989b) 'Base and Superstructure in Raymond Williams' in T. Eagleton (ed.) *Raymond Williams: Critical Perspectives*, Cambridge: Polity Press

—— (1989a) Introduction in T. Eagleton (ed.) *Raymond Williams: Critical Perspectives*, Cambridge: Polity Press

—— (1990) *The Ideology of the Aesthetic*, Oxford: Basil Blackwell

Easthope, A. (1991) *British Post-Structuralism Since 1968*, London: Routledge

Felperin, H. (1985) *Beyond Deconstruction: The Uses and Abuses of Literary Theory*, Oxford: Oxford University Press

Fiori, G. (1970) *Antonio Gramsci: Life of a Revolutionary*, trans. T. Nairn, London: New Left Books

Foucault, M. (1965) *Madness and Civilisation: A History of Insanity in the Age of Reason*, trans. R. Howard, New York: Vintage Books

—— (1972a) *Histoire de la folie à l'âge classique*, Paris: Gallimard

—— (1972b) *The Archaeology of Knowledge*, trans. A. M. Sheridan, London: Tavistock

—— (1973a) *The Birth of the Clinic*, trans. A. M. Sheridan, London: Tavistock

—— (1973b) *The Order of Things: An Archaeology of the Human Sciences*, New York: Vintage Books

—— (1977a) *Language, Counter-Memory, Practice*, trans. D. F. Bouchard and S. Simon, Ithaca: Cornell University Press

—— (1977b) *Discipline and Punish: The Birth of the Prison*, trans. A. M. Sheridan, Harmondsworth: Allen Lane

—— (1978) *The History of Sexuality*, trans. R. Hurley, New York: Random House

—— (1980) *Power/Knowledge: Selected Interviews and Other Writings, 1972-1977*, ed. C. Gordon, Brighton: Harvester Press

—— (1985) *The Use of Pleasure*, trans. R. Hurley, New York: Pantheon Books

Fox, R. (1979) *The Novel and the People*, London: Lawrence and Wishart

Frow, J. (1986) *Marxism and Literary History*, Oxford: Basil Blackwell

Garnham, N. (ed.) (1980) 'Class and Culture, the Work of Pierre Bourdieu' *Media, Culture and Society*, 2, 3

—— (1983) 'Towards a Theory of Cultural Materialism' *Journal of Communication*, 33, 3

—— (1986) 'Contribution to a Political Economy of Mass-communication' in R. Collins et al. (eds) *Media, Culture and Society: A Critical Reader*, London: Sage

—— (1988) 'Raymond Williams, 1921-1988: A Cultural Analyst, A Distinctive Tradition' *Journal of Communication* 38, 4

—— (1990) *Capitalism and Communication: Global Culture and the Economics of Information*, London: Sage

Garnham, N. and R. Williams (1986) 'Pierre Bourdieu and the Sociology of Culture' in R. Collins et al. *Media, Culture and Society: A Critical Reader*, London: Sage

Goldmann, L. (1964) *The Hidden God*, trans. P. Thody, London: Routledge & Kegan Paul

—— (1969) *The Human Sciences and Philosophy*, trans. H. V. White and R. Anchor, London: Jonathan Cape

—— (1971) *Immanuel Kant*, trans. R. Black, London: New Left Books

—— (1975) *Towards a Sociology of the Novel*, trans. A. Sheridan, London: Tavistock

Gramsci, A. (1957) *The Modern Prince and other Essays*, trans. L. Marks, London: Lawrence & Wishart

—— (1971) *Selections from Prison Notebooks*, trans. Q. Hoare and G. Nowell Smith, London: Lawrence & Wishart

Green, M. (1978) 'Raymond Williams and Cultural Studies' in P. Davison et al. (eds) *The Cultural Debate*, Part I, Cambridge: Chadwyck-Healey

Greenfield, C. and P. Williams (1989) 'Raymond Williams: The Political and Analytical Legacies' *Southern Review*, 22, 2

Grossberg, L. et al. (1988) *It's a Sin: Essays on Postmodernism, Politics and Culture*, Sydney: Power Publications

Habermas, J. (1971) *Knowledge and Human Interest*, trans. J. J. Shapiro, Boston: Beacon Press

—— (1979a) 'Interview with Jürgen Habermas' *New German Critique* 18

—— (1979b) 'Conservatism and Capitalist Crisis' *New Left Review* 115

—— (1981) 'New Social Movements' *Telos* 49

—— (1984) *The Theory of Communicative Action*, vol. 1, *Reason and the Rationalisation of Society*, trans. T. McCarthy, Boston: Beacon Press

—— (1985) 'Modernity — An Incomplete Project' trans. S. Ben-Habib, in H. Foster (ed.) *Postmodern Culture*, London: Pluto Press

—— (1987a) *The Philosophical Discourse of Modernity*, trans. F. Lawrence, Cambridge: Polity Press

—— (1987b) *The Theory of Communicative Action*, vol. 2 *Lifeworld and System: A Critique of Functionalist Reason*, trans. T. McCarthy, Cambridge: Polity Press

—— (1989) *The Structural Transformation of the Public Sphere*, trans. T. Burger, Cambridge: Polity Press

—— (1990) 'What Does Socialism Mean Today? The Rectifying Revolution and the Need for New Thinking on the Left', trans. B. Morgan, *New Left Review* 183

Hall, S. (1976) 'A Critical Survey of the Theoretical and Practical Achievements of the Last Ten Years' in F. Barker et al. (eds) *Literature, Society and the Sociology of Literature*, Colchester: Department of Literature, University of Essex

—— (1978) 'The Hinterland of Science: Ideology and The "Sociology of Knowledge" ' in Centre for Contemporary Cultural Studies, *On Ideology*, London: Hutchinson/Centre for Contemporary Cultural Studies

—— (1980a) 'Cultural Studies and the Centre: Some Problematics and Problems' in S. Hall et al. (eds) *Culture, Media, Language*, London: Hutchinson/Centre for Contemporary Cultural Studies

—— (1980b) 'Encoding/Decoding' in S. Hall et al. (eds) *Culture, Media, Language*, London: Hutchinson/Centre for Contemporary Cultural Studies

—— (1980c) 'Cultural Studies: Two Paradigms' *Media, Culture and Society* 2, 1

—— (1980d) 'The Williams Interviews' *Screen Education* 34

—— (1981) 'Cultural Studies: Two Paradigms' in T. Bennett et al. (eds) *Culture, Ideology and Social Process: A Reader*, London: Batsford Academic/Open University Press

—— (1983) 'The Great Moving Right Show' in S. Hall and M. Jacques (eds) *The Politics of Thatcherism*, London: Lawrence & Wishart

—— (1984) 'Face the Future' *New Socialist* September

—— (1986) 'Popular Culture and the State' in T. Bennett et al. (eds) *Popular Culture and Social Relations*, Milton Keynes: Open University Press

—— (1988a) 'The Toad in the Garden: Thatcherism among the Theorists' in C. Nelson and L. Grossberg (eds) *Marxism and the Interpretation of Culture*, London: Macmillan

—— (1988b) 'Thatcher's Lessons' *Marxism Today* March

—— (1989) 'Politics and Letters' in T. Eagleton (ed.) *Raymond Williams: Critical Perspectives*, Cambridge: Polity Press

—— (1991) Introduction in R. Simon, *Gramsci's Political Thought* second edn., London: Lawrence & Wishart

Hall, S. and T. Jefferson (eds) (1976) *Resistance Through Rituals: Youth Sub-cultures in Post-war Britain*, London: Hutchinson/Centre for Contemporary Cultural Studies

Hall, S. et al. (eds) (1968) *May Day Manifesto*, Harmondsworth: Penguin

—— (1978a) *Policing the Crisis: Mugging, the State, and Law and Order*, London: Macmillan

—— (1978b) 'Politics and Ideology: Gramsci' in Centre for Contemporary Cultural Studies, *On Ideology*, London: Hutchinson/Centre for Contemporary Cultural Studies

—— (eds) (1980) *Culture, Media Language*, London: Hutchinson/Centre for Contemporary Cultural Studies

Hampton, C. (1990) *The Ideology of the Text*, Milton Keynes: Open University Press

Hartman, G. (ed.) (1979) *Deconstruction and Criticism*, New York: Seabury Press

Hobbes, T. (1960) *Leviathan*, Oxford: Basil Blackwell

Hoggart, R. (1958) *The Uses of Literacy*, Harmondsworth: Penguin

—— (1970) *Speaking To Each Other, vol.2 About Literature*, London: Chatto & Windus

Hoggart, R. and R. Williams (1960) 'Working Class Attitudes' *New Left Review* 1

Hunter, I. (1988) *Culture and Government: The Emergence of Literary Education*, London: Macmillan

Johnson, L. (1987) 'Raymond Williams: a Marxist View of Culture' in D. Austin-Broos (ed.) *Creating Culture: Profiles in the Study of Culture*, Sydney: Allen & Unwin

—— (1988) *The Unseen Voice: A Cultural Study of Early Australian Radio*, London: Routledge

Johnson, R. (1979) 'Histories of Culture/Theories of Ideology: Notes on an Impasse' in M. Barrett et al. (eds) *Ideology and Cultural Production*, London: Croom Helm

Jones, P. (1982) ' "Organic" Intellectuals and the Generation of English Cultural Studies: An Introduction-to-cum-Historical-Survey-of The Field' *Thesis Eleven* 5/6

Koh, C.-Y. (1991), Back to the Future: The Critique of Postmodernism in Williams and Habermas, Monash University: BA Hons thesis

Kristeva, J. (1984) *Revolution in Poetic Language*, trans. M. Waller, New York: Columbia University Press

Lacan, J. (1977) *Écrits: A Selection*, trans. A. Sheridan, London: Tavistock

Laclau, E. (1977) *Politics and Ideology in Marxist Theory: Capitalism, Fascism, Populiam*, London: New Left Books

Laclau, E. and C. Mouffe (1988) *Hegemony and Socialist Strategy: Towards a Radical Democratic Politics*, London: Verso

Leavis, F. R. (1933) *For Continuity*, Cambridge: Minority Press

—— (1938) *New Bearings in English Poetry*, London: Chatto & Windus

—— (1948) *Education and the University: A Sketch for an 'English School'*, London: Chatto & Windus

—— (1962a) *The Common Pursuit*, Harmondsworth: Penguin

—— (1962b) *The Great Tradition*, Harmondsworth: Penguin

—— (1962c) *Two Cultures?*, London: Chatto & Windus

—— (1963) *'Scrutiny*: A Retrospect' *Scrutiny* 20

—— (1972a) *Nor Shall My Sword*, London: Chatto & Windus

—— (1972b) *Revaluation*, Harmondsworth: Penguin

Leavis, F. R. and D.Thompson (1960) *Culture and Environment*, London: Chatto & Windus

Leavis, Q. D. (1979) *Fiction and the Reading Public*, Harmondsworth: Penguin

Lentricchia, F. (1980) *After the New Criticism*, Chicago: University of Chicago Press

Lévi-Strauss, C. (1972) *Structural Anthropology*, trans. C. Jacobson and B. Grundfest Schoepf, Harmondsworth: Penguin

Levy, B. (1989) 'Speaking a "Committed" Position: Work in Process' *Southern Review*, 22, 2

Lovell, T. (1980) *Pictures of Reality: Aesthetics, Politics, Pleasure*, London: British Film Institute

—— (1987) *Consuming Fiction*, London: Verso

—— (1989) 'Knowable Pasts, Imaginable Futures' *History Workshop* 27

Lukács, G. (1962) *The Historical Novel*, trans. H. and S. Mitchell, London: Merlin Press

—— (1963) *The Meaning of Contemporary Realism*, trans. J. and N. Mander, London: Merlin Press

—— (1971a) *History and Class Consciousness*, trans. R. Livingstone, London: Merlin Press

—— (1971b) *The Theory of the Novel*, trans. A. Bostock, London: Merlin Press

MacCabe, C. (1978) *James Joyce and the Revolution of the Word*, London: Macmillan

—— (1985) *Theoretical Essays: Film, Linguistics, Literature*, Manchester: Manchester University Press

MacDermott, K. (1983) 'The Discourse of Assessment. English Studies at Melbourne University' *Melbourne Working Papers* 4

Macherey, P. (1978) *A Theory of Literary Production*, trans. G. Wall, London: Routledge & Kegan Paul

Marx, K. (1970) *Capital* vol.1, trans. S. Moore and E. Aveling, London: Lawrence & Wishart

—— (1975) *Early Writings*, Harmondsworth: Penguin

Marx, K. and F. Engels (1947) *Literature and Art*, New York: International Publishers

Merleau-Ponty, M. (1974) *Adventures of the Dialectic*, trans. J. Bien, London: Heinemann

Merrington, J. (1968) 'Theory and Practice in Gramsci's Marxism' in R. Miliband and J. Saville (eds) *The Socialist Register 1968*, London: Merlin Press

Mitchell, J. (1966) 'Women: The Longest Revolution' *New Left Review* 40

Mouffe, C. (ed.) (1979) *Gramsci and Marxist Theory*, London: Routledge & Kegan Paul

Mulhern, F. (1981) *The Moment of 'Scrutiny'*, London: Verso

O'Connor, A. (1989) *Raymond Williams: Writing, Culture, Politics*, Oxford: Basil Blackwell

O'Connor, J. and S. Redhead (1991) Book Review , *Theory, Culture and Society* 8, 4

Oxford English Limited (1989) Editorial: 'Third Generation' *News From Nowhere* 6

Parsons, T. (1949) *The Structure of Social Action*, New York: Free Press

Plekhanov, G. (1956) *The Development of the Monist View of History*, trans. A. Rothstein, Moscow: Foreign Languages Publishing House

—— (1978) 'Art and Social Life' trans. E. Hartley et al. in P. Davison et al. (eds.) *Art and Social Life*, Cambridge: Chadwyck Healey

Pinkney, T. (1989) 'Raymond Williams and the "Two Faces of Modernism" ' in T. Eagleton (ed.) *Raymond Williams: Critical Perspectives*, Cambridge: Polity Press

Radek, K. (1977) 'Contemporary World Literature and the Tasks of Proletarian Art' in M. Gorky et al. *Soviet Writers' Congress 1934: The Debate on Socialist Realism and Modernism*, London: Lawrence & Wishart

Robey, D. (ed.) (1973) *Structuralism: An Introduction*, Oxford: Oxford University Press

Rowbotham, S. (1985) 'Picking up the Pieces' *New Socialist*, October

Sartre, J.-P. (1950) *What is Literature?*, trans. B. Frechtman, London: Methuen

—— (1976) *Critique of Dialectical Reason*, trans. A. Sheridan-Smith, London: New Left Books

—— (1976–1977) 'Socialism in One Country' *New Left Review*, 100

Saussure, F. de (1974) *Course in General Linguistics*, trans. W. Baskin, Glasgow: Fontana

Sedgwick, P. (1976) 'The Two New Lefts' in D. Widgery (ed.) *The Left in Britain 1956-1968*, Harmondsworth: Penguin

Shelley, P. B. (1931) *A Defence of Poetry* (with P. Sidney *An Apology for Poetry*), ed. H. A. Needham, London: Ginn & Co.

Sinfield, A. (1983) 'Literary Theory and the "Crisis" in English Studies' *Critical Quarterly* 25, 3

—— (1989) *Literature, Politics and Culture in Postwar Britain*, Oxford: Basil Blackwell

Sparks, C. (1980) 'Raymond Williams, Culture and Marxism' *International Socialism* 2nd series, 9

Thompson, E. P. (1955) *William Morris: Romantic to Revolutionary*, London: Lawrence & Wishart

—— (1957) 'Socialist Humanism: An Epistle to the Philistines' *New Reasoner* 1

—— (1963) *The Making of the English Working Class*, London: Victor Gollancz

—— (1977) 'Postscript 1976', *William Morris: Romantic to Revolutionary*, second edn., London: Merlin Press

—— (1978) *The Poverty of Theory and Other Essays*, London: Merlin Press

Tönnies, F. (1955) *Community and Association*, trans. C. P. Loomis, London: Routledge & Kegan Paul

Trotsky, L. (1970) *On Literature and Art*, ed. P. N. Siegel, New York: Pathfinder Press

Turner, G. (1990) *British Cultural Studies: An Introduction*, London: Unwin Hyman

Volosinov, V. N. (1973) *Marxism and the Philosophy of Language*, trans. L. Matejka and I. R. Titunik, New York: Seminar Press

Waites, B. et al. (eds) (1982) *Popular Culture: Past and Present*, London: Croom Helm/Open University Press

Watts, C. (1989) 'Reclaiming the Border Country: Feminism and Raymond Williams' *News From Nowhere* 6

Weber, M. (1948) *From Max Weber: Essays in Sociology*, ed. H. H. Gerth and C. W. Mills, London: Routledge & Kegan Paul

—— (1964) *The Theory of Social and Economic Organization*, trans. A. M. Henderson and T. Parsons, New York: Free Press

Wellek, R. (1937) 'Literary Criticism and Philosophy' *Scrutiny* 5, 4

West, A. (1975) *Crisis and Criticism*, London: Lawrence & Wishart

Widdowson, P. (1982) 'The Crisis in English Studies' in P. Widdowson (ed.) *Re-Reading English*, London: Methuen

Williams, R. (1952) *Drama from Ibsen to Eliot*, London: Chatto & Windus

—— (1958) 'Culture is Ordinary' in N. Mackenzie (ed) *Conviction*, London: MacGibbon & Kee

—— (1960) *Border Country*, London: Chatto & Windus

—— (1962) *Communications*, Harmondsworth: Penguin

—— (1963) *Culture and Society 1780-1950*, Harmondsworth: Penguin (first published London, Chatto & Windus, 1958)

—— (1964) *Second Generation*, London: Chatto & Windus

—— (1965) *The Long Revolution*, Harmondsworth: Penguin (first published London, Chatto & Windus, 1961)

—— (1966) *Modern Tragedy*, London: Chatto & Windus

—— (1968) *Drama in Performance*, second edn., London: C. A. Watts

—— (1971a) *George Orwell*, New York: Viking Press

—— (1971b) 'Literature and Sociology: In Memory of Lucien Goldmann' *New Left Review* 67

—— (1972) *Gesellschaftstheorie als Begriffsgeschichte: Studien z. histor. Semantik von Kultur,* trans. Dt. von Heinz Blumensath, Munich: Rogner & Bernhard

—— (1973a) *Drama from Ibsen to Brecht,* Harmondsworth: Penguin (first published London, Chatto & Windus, 1968)

—— (1973b) *The Country and the City,* New York: Oxford University Press

—— (1973c) 'Base and Superstructure in Marxist Cultural Theory' *New Left Review* 82

—— (1974a) *The English Novel: From Dickens to Lawrence,* St Albans: Paladin (first published London, Chatto & Windus, 1970)

—— (1974b) *Television: Technology and Cultural Form,* Glasgow: Fontana

—— (1976a) Keywords: *A Vocabulary of Culture and Society,* Glasgow: Fontana

—— (1976b) *Communications,* third edn., Harmondsworth: Penguin

—— (1977a) *Marxism and Literature* Oxford: Oxford University Press

—— (1977b) 'Forms of English Fiction in 1848' in F. Barker et al. (eds) *1848: The Sociology of Literature,* Colchester: Department of Literature, University of Essex

—— (1978a) 'Problems of Materialism' *New Left Review* 109

—— (1978b) *The Volunteers,* London: Eyre Methuen

—— (1979a) *Politics and Letters: Interviews with New Left Review,* London: New Left Books

—— (1979b) *Modern Tragedy,* second edn., London: Verso

—— (1979c) *The Fight for Manod,* London: Chatto & Windus

—— (1980) *Problems in Materialism and Culture: Selected Essays,* London: New Left Books

—— (1981) *Culture,* Glasgow: Fontana

—— (1983) *Towards 2000,* London: Chatto & Windus

—— (1984a) 'Seeing a Man Running' in D. Thompson (ed.) *The Leavises: Recollections and Impressions,* Cambridge: Cambridge University Press

—— (1984b) *Writing in Society,* London: Verso

—— (1985) *Loyalties*, London: Chatto & Windus

—— (1989a) *The Politics of Modernism: Against the New Conformists*, ed. T. Pinkney, London: Verso

—— (1989b) *Resources of Hope: Culture, Democracy, Socialism*, ed. R. Gable, London: Verso

—— (1989c) *What I Came To Say*, ed. N. Belton et al., London: Hutchinson Radius

Williams, R. and M. Orrom (1954) *Preface to Film*, London: Film Drama

Wolff, J. (1981) *The Social Production of Art*, London: Macmillan

—— (1990) *Feminine Sentences: Essays on Women and Culture*, Cambridge: Polity Press

Women's Studies Group (1978) *Women Take Issue: Aspects of Women's Subordination*, London: Hutchinson/Centre for Contemporary Cultural Studies

Wordsworth, W. (1952) *The Poetical Works of William Wordsworth*, Oxford: Oxford University Press

Zhdanov, A. A. (1977) 'Soviet Literature—The Richest in Ideas, the Most Advanced in Literature' in M. Gorky et al. *Soviet Writers' Congress 1934: The Debate on Socialist Realism and Modernism*, London: Lawrence & Wishart

Index